TUNING IN

Listening and Speaking in the Real World

Carol Numrich

PEARSON
Longman

Tuning In: Listening and Speaking in the Real World

Pearson Education, 10 Bank St., White Plains, NY 10606

Vice president, multimedia and skills:
   Sherri Preiss
Executive editor, higher education: Laura Le Dréan
Associate acquistions editor: Amy
   McCormick
Development editor: Debbie Sistino
Director of editorial production: Linda Moser
Production manager: Christine Edmonds
Production editor: Leigh Stolle
Director of manufacturing: Patrice Fraccio

Senior manufacturing buyer:
   Nancy Flaggman
Cover and text design: Pat Wosczyk
Cover image: Marjory Dressler
   Photo Graphics
Photo research: Shana McGuire
Illustrations: Jill Wood
Text composition: Laserwords
Text font: 10/13 New Aster
Text and photo credits: see p.168.

Reviewers: Linda Pelc, LaGuardia Community College, New York, NY; Linda Wells, University of Washington, Seattle, WA; Gail Fingado, Columbia University, New York, NY; Kathy Sherak, American Language Institute, San Francisco, CA; Milie Stoff, MiamiDade Community College, Miami, FL.

Library of Congress Cataloging-in-Publication Data

Numrich, Carol.
   Tuning in/Carol Numrich.
      p.cm.
Includes bibliographical references and index.
Summary: A listening/speaking textbook design for low-intermediate students with two distinguishing features: completely authentic listening material, and significant use of inference-level comprehension questions.
ISBN 0-13-191932-6 (student book : alk. paper) — ISBN 0-13-193267-5 (audio CDs)—
ISBN 0-13-193268-3 (answer key : alk. paper)
   1.   English language—Textbooks for foreign speakers. 2. English language—
Spoken English—Problems, exercises, etc. 3. Listening—Problems,
exercises, etc. I. Title.
PE1128.N853 2006
428.3'4—dc22

2005013870

ISBN: 0-13-191932–6

Printed in the United States of America
4 5 6 7 8 9 10—BAH—10 09

Contents

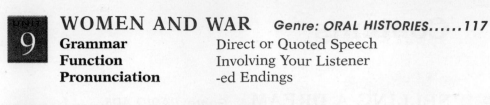

Introduction

Tuning In: Listening and Speaking in the Real World is designed for intermediate level students of English. The text contains 30 authentic, carefully selected listening segments ranging from commercials to interviews to love songs. Students are keenly aware of the difference between listening material that has been prepared for their student ears and listening material that has been prepared for native speaker ears.

Tuning In gives students at this level a unique opportunity to engage with listening material from the real world.

The text consists of 10 units each focusing on a genre of listening as well as a particular theme. For example, each of the three listening segments in Unit 3 is a monologue in which a man recalls memories from his childhood. The corresponding activities emphasize critical thinking skills including inference, synthesis, and analysis. In the Looking at Language section, different aspects of spoken language—pronunciation, grammar, and function—are highlighted and practiced. In the Wrap Up section, students review and synthesize ideas from the three listening segments. Then, through analysis and creation activities, they gain a deeper understanding of the structure of the listening and have a chance to create their own works related to the theme and listening genre of the unit.

Unit Organization and Suggestions for Use

The exercises are designed to stimulate an interest in the material by drawing on students' previous knowledge and opinions and by aiding comprehension through vocabulary and guided listening exercises.

Each unit is divided into sections corresponding to the three listening segments. Each section begins with an interesting visual and a brief introduction. Discussion questions prepare students for the content of the listening. Students work in small groups to discuss their answers to these questions. Alternatively, the questions might be used for a class discussion.

A Vocabulary Preview
In this section, a variety of exercises is presented to prepare students for vocabulary and expressions used in the listening selection. Exercises include guessing meaning from sentence or whole-text contexts, reading definitions of words and phrases and then using them in sentences, mini-dialogs, or whole text contexts, and matching pictures with definitions.

B Listening for the Main Ideas
Students listen to the segment the first time for the main ideas and answer questions. Only one listening is usually required in Listening for the Main Ideas; however, some classes may want to listen twice in order to ensure comprehension of the important information.

C **Listening for Details**

Here students are asked to focus on detailed information. They first read through the exercise, and then listen to the segment again as they complete the exercise, thus actively evaluating their comprehension. Activities include fill-ins, true/false, multiple choice, short answers, matching, and sequencing. Then, in pairs, students compare answers. The teacher should encourage the students to defend their answers. There will certainly be disagreements over some of the answers, and these discussions will help focus attention on the information needed to answer the questions correctly. By listening for details a second time, the students generally recognize this information. Once again, they should be asked to compare their answers. If there are still misunderstandings, the segment might be played a third time with the teacher verifying the answers.

D **Listening for Inference**

In this section, students are asked to listen to short excerpts from the listening segment again in order to infer or interpret the attitudes, feelings, points of view, or intended meanings of the speakers. To do this they might focus on speakers' tone of voice, stress and intonation patterns, or choice of language. Students may express slightly varied interpretations in their answers. This is to be expected, since inference can be subjective. For this reason, there are *suggested answers* in the Answer Key. Any varying answers and differences in interpretation can be a good opportunity for interesting class discussion.

E **Discussion**

After working on listening comprehension, students work in groups to discuss questions related to the listening segments. Here, students are invited to express their opinions in light of the information they have heard. They will most likely have different points of view and should be encouraged to present their differing views to each other.

F **Looking at Language**

In each unit, three different aspects of spoken language are highlighted: *pronunciation, functional language,* and *grammar.* Each listening segment focuses on one of the three aspects of particular interest in the segment, either because of its frequent use or because of its importance in comprehending the listening segment. Students first examine the language point as it occurs naturally in the listening segment. They make guesses about rules, usage or meaning. Then they read explanations with examples. Finally, they practice the language point in an oral or written exercise.

Wrap up

The purpose of the Wrap Up section is to tie together the three listening segments from the unit. The teacher may want to do one, two or all three of these activities.

A **Synthesis**

In the Synthesis activities, students work in groups to combine, compare and contrast, or examine more closely language and/or concepts from the three listening segments. Students should work in small groups to share their ideas and complete the task together.

B **Analysis**

In Analysis activities, students examine the nuts and bolts of the genre of listening focused on in the unit. Students consider the structure or purpose of a particular point: Where do the songwriters or poets use rhyme? Where does a commercial use humor to get a listener's attention? What is the problem/solution structure in the stories or in the chefs' cooking tips? After completing the Analysis activities, students are better prepared to do the Creation activity that follows.

C **Creation**

In the final phase of the unit, students are invited to create their own work related to the theme and listening genre of the unit. They work in pairs, groups or individually to create their own monologues, dialogues, or interviews. They also write their own songs, stories, or commercials, using language and concepts that were presented in the unit. The teacher may want to encourage students to record their work and give audio presentations to the class.

Acknowledgments

Many people are to be acknowledged for their help in developing this text. First and foremost, the research and development for this project would not have been possible without the pedagogical leave that was granted to me by my colleagues on the Standing Committee of Language Lecturers at Columbia University in the spring of 2004. I am grateful to them and to David Quinn, the chair of the American Language Program, for supporting my work.

Several of my colleagues at the American Language Program provided valuable feedback on the material. I am grateful to Frances Boyd, Judy Miller, Milena Remis, and Barbara Sarapata for piloting material in their classes and providing helpful feedback. I am also indebted to Linda Lane for advising me on pronunciation and Gail Fingado for her detailed review of the text and helpful suggestions. Thanks also to Martha Cummings and Peg Hazenbush for providing ideas for my poetry unit.

This project also involved the help and support of many people during the research process. I am indebted to Joe Donahue, News Director at WAMC, for helping me obtain call-in segments on pet advice, and to Sue Sternberg and Jon Katz for their contributions. I am thankful to Maiken Scott, of WHYY, for helping with permissions for "A Chef's Table," and Ed Keyes, President of World Talk Radio, for providing excerpts from "The Chef Larry Show," and "Gourmet Table." Diane Vogel, of WAMU, was instrumental in clearing permissions and providing contacts with storytellers. Thanks also to the storytellers and writers Diane Macklin, Howard Schwartz, Mark Novak, Renee Brachfeld, and Marc Spiegel for sharing their work. Anneliesa Clump and Lee Woodman, from the Veterans History Project in Washington D.C., helped me obtain permissions and contacts for oral history excerpts. I would like to express special thanks to Jeanne Markle, Marion Gurfein, and Tomika Perdomo for their war memory contributions. Chris Doyle, John Tierney, and Janine Quatreving were very helpful in getting radio commercials for this project. Jeffrey Rosenberg, of Rosenberg Communications, Inc., made it possible to include award-winning PSAs in the text. David Greenberger and Martin Jacobson were wonderfully willing to share their boyhood stories. David Roth, a very dear friend, connected me to his world of music. Special thanks go to David, Cozy Sheridan, and Lui Collins for sharing their love songs with a new international audience.

Finally, I owe much to my editors at Longman. Sherry Preiss, a key person in this project, offered me ideas, contacts, and helpful research tips. Without Sherry, this project could not have been realized. Laura Le Dréan helped guide the conceptualization. I am so appreciative of her steadfast, dependable role in offering insights and moving things forward. Debbie Sistino helped mold my work into a more succinct text. She is a terrific editor! Thanks, too, to Leigh Stolle, the Production Editor; Dana Klinek for all her hard work securing permissions; and Shana McGuire for her tireless efforts researching visual material.

Selling a Dream

Genre: RADIO ADS

What is your favorite radio ad? What do you like about it?

Every day we hear advertising on the radio or television. Successful ads use clever ways to get the attention of listeners. Many ads are entertaining. Often they are funny. They sometimes have music or background noises to get our attention. They often have people talking about their experience with a product. All these techniques help sell the product.

The three radio ads you will hear in this unit share some of these techniques.

LISTENING 1: An ad for The New York State Lottery

LISTENING 2: An ad for Okemo Ski Resort

LISTENING 3: An ad for Cupid.com

Work in groups. Discuss your answers to the following questions.

1. Have you ever played a lottery?

2. Do you know anyone who has ever won a lottery?

Ⓐ Vocabulary Preview

Read the following sentences. Guess the meaning of the underlined words. Then choose a definition or synonym for each word.

1. Jerry is so happy. He played the lottery and won <u>a ton</u> of money!
  a. a small amount
  b. a lot

2. I have <u>zero</u> cents in my pocket! I've spent all my money today.
  a. 100
  b. 0

3. My brother-in-law is a <u>millionaire</u>. He got most of his money from his parents.
  a. very rich person
  b. very poor person

4. My uncle went to the party looking so handsome and <u>debonair</u>.
  a. dirty
  b. fashionable

5. Some people say the best part of a marriage is the <u>honeymoon</u>, when the marriage is so new.
  a. vacation taken after a wedding
  b. period of separation before a divorce

6. Joe was feeling <u>mighty</u> rich after he won the lottery.
  a. hardly
  b. very

7. She is so <u>tan</u> because she and her husband spent the summer at the beach.
  a. with dark skin
  b. with light skin

8. After spending all winter working in an office, Megan looked very <u>pale</u>.
  a. with dark skin
  b. with light skin

9. Gabe decided to give a <u>mega</u> party this year. He has invited everyone he knows!
  a. very small
  b. very big

B Listening for the Main Ideas

Listen to the ad. Which of the following best expresses the main idea of the ad? Circle the answer. Discuss your answer with a partner.

In this ad, Jen and Ben ____.

    a. played the lottery but didn't win any money

    b. played the lottery and won a lot of money

    c. didn't play the lottery and could have won a lot of money

C Listening for Details

Listen to the ad again. Fill in the missing words or phrases. Use words from Section A. Compare your answers with those of another student.

NEW YORK STATE LOTTERY AD
Come and listen to our story 'bout a girl named Jen
Livin' upstate with her husband named Ben.
Then one day when she stopped to get some gas
She picked the winning numbers,
And she won (**1**) ____ ____ ____ cash.
(Millions that is . . . lots of (**2**) _____!)

Well the next thing you know
Young Jen's a (**3**) _____,
Ben's got new clothes and he's lookin' (**4**) _____.
Told the travel agent "Gotta get away soon,"
So they jumped on a plane to their second (**5**) _____.
(And then a third . . . and a fourth after that!)

Now Ben and Jen are lookin' mighty (**6**) _____,
Smiling ear to ear, and walkin' hand-in-hand.
Say they can't believe just how (**7**) _____ they used to be
'til they got the winning numbers in the New York Lottery.

New York Lotto. New York's (**8**) _____-millions! It
can happen, ya hear?

For New York Lottery winning results, call 1-900-336-2020.
Calls are 40 cents a minute. Call 1-900-336-2020.

D Listening for Inference

Listen to the excerpt from the ad. Then answer the following questions. Discuss your answers with a partner.

    1. Why are Ben and Jen looking tan?

    2. How do they feel now? What do their ears and hands show us?

    3. Why did Ben and Jen used to be pale? What kind of life did they have before?

E Discussion

Work in groups. Discuss your answers to the following questions.

1. This ad gives the impression that winning the lottery will have a positive effect on a couple's life. Can you imagine any negative effects for couples who suddenly become millionaires?

2. Would you play the lottery? Why or why not?

F Looking at Language

Pronunciation: Plurals and Present Tense Endings

1. *Read the excerpt from the ad as you listen to it. What is the ending pronunciation of the highlighted words? One word has a different ending sound. Which one?*

> Come and listen to our story 'bout a girl named Jen
> Livin' upstate with her husband named Ben.
> Then one day when she stopped to get some gas
> She picked the winning **numbers**,
> And she won a ton of cash.
> (**Millions** that is . . . **lots** of **zeros**!)

In English, regular plurals and third person singular present verbs end in an -*s*. This final -*s* has three different pronunciations: /z/, /s/, and /əz/ or /ɪz/.

/z/ Pronounce the -*s* as /z/ when a word ends in a voiced sound (/b/, /d/, /g/, /v/, /r/, /l/, /m/, /n/, /ŋz/, /ð/, a vowel, or /w/ and /y/. All the words in the excerpt above (with the exception of *lots*) end with the /z/ sound.

Present Tense Endings	**Plurals**
Ben <u>knows</u> he looks debonair.	Jen and Ben had four <u>honeymoons</u>.
Jen now <u>gives</u> her hand to Ben.	Jen and Ben now love holding <u>hands</u>.
Jen <u>hopes</u> she <u>wins</u> again.	There are many state <u>lotteries</u> in the United States.

/s/ Pronounce the -*s* as /s/ when a word ends in a voiceless consonant (/p/, /t/, /k/ or /θ/). *Lots* in the excerpt above is an example of the /s/ ending.

Present Tense Endings	**Plurals**
He <u>hopes</u> to win the lottery.	She bought two lottery <u>tickets</u>.
Jen <u>picks</u> lucky numbers.	Call for winning <u>results</u>.
Now Ben <u>wants</u> to play the lottery.	Jen won big <u>bucks</u>!

əz/ or /ɪz/ When a word ends in /s/, /z/, /ʃ/, /tʃ/, /ʒ/, or /dʒ/, the -*s* ending is pronounced as an extra syllable: /əz/ or /ɪz/.

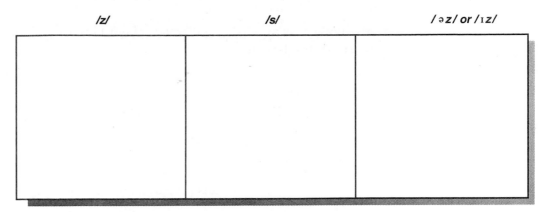

Present Tense Endings	Plurals
Jen's friend <u>wishes</u> she had won.	Jen had no <u>losses</u>.
Jen <u>judges</u> the right time to play lotto.	Ben has been to many <u>beaches</u>.
Now Jen never <u>misses</u> the chance to play.	Jen will get many <u>prizes</u>.

2. *Look at the transcript for the New York Lottery ad on page 149. Circle all the plural nouns. (There are 10.) In the chart below, categorize them according to their ending sound. One box will have no example.*

/z/	/s/	/ ə z/ or /ɪz/

3. *Compare your answers with those of another student. Then practice reading the words aloud to each other. Focus on the ending sounds.*

LISTENING 2 | OKEMO SKI RESORT AD

Work in groups. Discuss your answers to the following questions.

What is your ideal vacation? Where would you go and what would you do?

Ⓐ Vocabulary Preview

Read the following sentences. Use the underlined words to complete the definitions below.

a. Each year there are fewer skis and more <u>snowboards</u> at the ski resorts.

b. Let's not ski down this mountain. It hasn't been <u>groomed</u> since last night's snowfall.

c. Joe's father knows how to <u>sculpt</u> ice into beautiful designs.

d. Many people would like to go to outer space just to experience no <u>gravity</u>.

e. I hope we'll have a beautiful weekend, but we'll have to see what <u>Mother Nature</u> brings us.

f. My mother always <u>dishes out</u> advice about how I should live my life when I don't want to hear it.

g. I really wanted to buy those new skis this year, but they were too expensive. I guess I will have to <u>settle for</u> used ones.

h. Ever since the baby was born, the dog has felt <u>neglected</u> by the family.

i. The child <u>disrespected</u> his parents when he didn't obey their rules.

1. _____ means prepared an area for a certain activity.

2. _____ is the force that causes something to fall to the ground.

3. _____ are long wide boards that people use to ride down snow-covered mountains.

4. _____ refers to the force that controls and organizes the Earth, its weather, and the living creatures and plants on it.

5. _____ means not given enough attention.

6. To _____ is to carve or cut a solid object into a particular shape.

7. _____ means did not give respect.

8. To _____ is to accept or agree to something that is not what you want.

9. To _____ is to give something that is unwanted.

B Listening for the Main Ideas

Listen to the ad. Answer the following question. Discuss your answer with a partner.

Why is Okemo Ski Resort a great place to ski and snowboard?
- **a.** It snows there more than at other ski resorts.
- **b.** Snow groomers make the snow perfect for skiers and snowboarders.
- **c.** It's a great family place to snowboard and ski.

C Listening for Details

Listen to the ad again. Check (✓) the statements that are mentioned in the ad. Compare your answers with those of another student.

____ **1.** Okemo Mountain is in Vermont.

____ **2.** Okemo has the best conditions in the East.

____ **3.** Groomers were up all night grooming snow.

____ **4.** Aunt Tilly skis at night.

____ **5.** Snow has been groomed wall-to-wall.

____ **6.** Okemo can make snow into great conditions.

____ **7.** We need to settle for snow that's been neglected and disrespected.

____ **8.** Okemo treats snow like white gold.

D Listening for Inference

Read the excerpts from the ad as you listen to them. Several expressions are slang. Use the context to understand their meaning. Then answer the following questions. Discuss your answers with a partner.

"**Sick** pipe, **dude**."
"If you say so, dude."

So, whatever **Mother Nature dishes out**, Okemo can take it and make it into conditions that leave you feeling like this: *(people shouting happily)*

1. What does *sick* mean in this excerpt?
   a. great   **b.** unhealthy   **c.** dangerous

2. What does *dude* mean in this excerpt?
   a. bad guy   **b.** cool guy   **c.** young guy

3. What does the speaker mean by *Mother Nature* in this excerpt?

    a. your mother   **b.** the owner of   **c.** the weather
                                Okemo Ski Resort

4. What might Mother Nature *dish out*, according to this excerpt?

    a. warm weather   **b.** cold weather   **c.** snowstorms

E Discussion

Work in groups. Discuss your answers to the following questions.

1. How does this ad sell the Okemo Ski Resort? Would you go there after listening to this commercial?

2. Have you ever gone skiing? What is the best ski resort you have been to? Why did you like it?

F Looking at Language

Grammar: *-ing* and *-ed* Adjectives

1. *Read the excerpt from the Okemo Ski Resort ad. Notice the endings of the adjectives. Why do some adjectives in English end in **-ing**? Why do some adjectives end in **-ed**? How do these endings change meaning?*

That's the sound of riders in the Okemo super pipe performing their gravity-defy**ing** deeds of daring on snow groom**ed** wall-to-wall.

When *-ing* forms are used as adjectives, they have similar meaning to active verbs:

    gravity-<u>defying</u> deeds = deeds that <u>defy</u> gravity

When *-ed* forms are used as adjectives, they have similar meaning to passive verbs:

    <u>groomed</u> snow = snow that <u>has been groomed</u>

We use *-ing* forms to describe the people or things that cause feelings:

    My ski lesson was so <u>boring</u>.
    The rain during our ski trip was really <u>depressing</u>.

We use *-ed* forms to describe how people feel:

    I didn't enjoy my ski lesson because I was so <u>bored</u>.
    I felt <u>depressed</u> when it started to rain during our ski trip.

---

2. *Work in pairs. Student A reads a statement. Student B reads the response with either the **-ing** or **-ed** adjective. Student A corrects Student B's answer if necessary. Change roles after item 5. (Student A, look at this page. Student B, look at page 148.)*

Student A

1. What did you think of that ski lesson?   (Answer: *interested*)

2. How did you like snowboarding down that pipe, dude?   (Answer: *exciting*)

3. Would you like to spend a week skiing here? (Answer: *bored*)

4. Why haven't you gone skiing these last few years? (Answer: *depressing*)

5. Don't you feel great after a day of snowboarding? (Answer: *tiring*)

6. Oh, I'm completely (satisfying/satisfied)!

7. You're right! He is truly (amazing/amazed)!

8. I am so (surprising/surprised). I was sure that I couldn't make it down without falling!

9. It was just beautiful. I was so (moving/moved).

10. Yes! He was very (amusing/amused) and kept the students laughing all day.

LISTENING 3　**CUPID.COM AD**

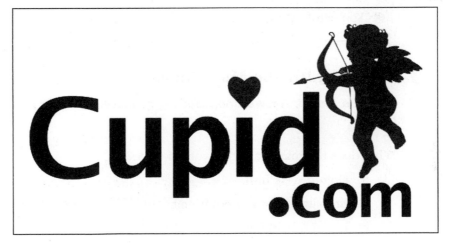

Work in groups. Discuss your answers to the following questions.

1. Have you ever tried to meet someone through an Internet dating service?
2. Do you think it's a good way to find the perfect man or woman?

Vocabulary Preview

*Read the definitions of the following words and phrases. Then complete the
sentences with the best word or phrase.*

be negative:	focus on only the bad qualities of a situation or person
getting on (someone's) nerves:	annoying someone, especially by doing something again and again
cute as a button:	very attractive; adorable
browse:	look for and find information on the Internet
skip:	not do something on purpose
brighter:	smarter

1. Gerry didn't do very well in school; his brothers were much
_____ than he was.

2. Look at the baby in her new coat. She's just _____!

3. My sister tends to _____. She is never happy with her life.

4. We already saw the beginning of this movie, so let's _____ the
first part.

5. My neighbor keeps parking his car in front of my driveway. He's really
_____!

6. You can find any information you need these days. Just go online and
_____!

Ⓑ **Listening for the Main Ideas**

*Listen to the ad. Answer the following question. Discuss your answer with a
partner.*

What does the man want the woman to do?

   a. Go out with him.

   b. Stop looking for a boyfriend.

   c. Let him help her find a date.

C Listening for Details

Listen to the ad again. Fill in the missing information. Compare your answers with those of another student.

1. Somewhere on this _____ _____, there's someone looking for you.

2. The man thinks the woman is being _____ and that there is someone for her.

3. The man tells the woman she is getting on his _____ when she keeps questioning him.

4. The woman thinks the man in the car next to her is _____.

5. The man wants to know why the woman keeps on _____ things.

6. At Cupid.com you can _____ thousands of people in your area.

7. Registration is _____.

8. The man has _____ thousand other men and women to talk to.

9. The man _____ telling the men, "That's a nice skirt you're wearing."

10. The man hopes that his next client will be a little _____.

D Listening for Inference

Listen to the excerpt from the ad. Then answer the following question. Discuss your answer with a partner.

Does the woman think there is someone out there for her?

E Discussion

Work in groups. Discuss your answers to the following questions.

1. What is your reaction to this ad? Is it funny? What do you think about the man's attitude? What do you think about the woman's attitude?

2. What are the advantages and disadvantages of Internet dating? Do you know people who met on the Internet?

⒡ Looking at Language

Function: Expressing Doubt

🎧 1. *Read Excerpt 1 as you listen to it. Then read and listen to Excerpt 2. Focus on the highlighted phrases. What attitude do they express? Which phrase seems to express the attitude most strongly?*

Excerpt 1

Man: Somewhere on this radio station, out in the ether, there's someone looking for you.

Woman: **Yeah, right**.

Man: Don't be so negative. There is someone just for you.

Woman: Me?

Man: Yes, you.

Woman: **Really**?

Man: Yes.

Woman: **Really and truly**?

Excerpt 2

Man: Cupid.com. Registration is free, and no one knows who you are until you want them to know who you are.

Woman: **Sounds too good to be true!**

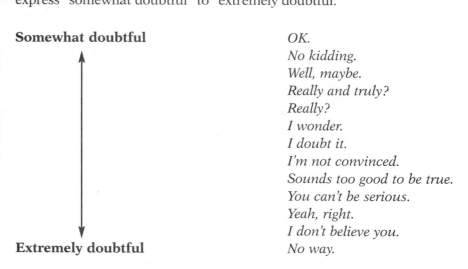

In the excerpts above, the woman expresses doubt. She doesn't believe that there is a man for her. She wonders whether the Cupid.com service can really be helpful. In the excerpts above, "Yeah, right" is the most doubtful expression. There are many phrases we use to express doubt. We can express "somewhat doubtful" to "extremely doubtful."

Somewhat doubtful

↕

Extremely doubtful

OK.
No kidding.
Well, maybe.
Really and truly?
Really?
I wonder.
I doubt it.
I'm not convinced.
Sounds too good to be true.
You can't be serious.
Yeah, right.
I don't believe you.
No way.

2. *Work in pairs to write mini-dialogues. First review the examples. Complete each dialogue using a comment with a doubtful response from the list above. Then end with another comment. Be sure that the final comment responds to the level of doubt of the response you use from the list. Read your dialogues aloud to the class.*

EXAMPLES

A: That's a nice skirt you're wearing.
B: *Really?* It's 10 years old!
A: Well, I think it looks great on you.

A: I know you're going to meet the man of your life.
B: *No way!* It will never happen.
A: Well, maybe you won't meet him if you have *that* attitude!

1. A: I think there's someone for everyone.

    B: _____

    A: _____

2. A: Look at her. She's beautiful!

    B: _____

    A: _____

3. A: If you browse the Internet, you can meet great people.

    B: _____

    A: _____

4. A: I went on my first date with him. He's so smart!

    B: _____

    A: _____

5. A: Hey! You look great today.

    B: _____

    A: _____

6. A: I think your son is as cute as a button!

    B: _____

    A: _____

7. A: Call her. I know she would love to hear from you.

    B: _____

    A: _____

WRAP UP

Ⓐ Synthesis

The purpose of an ad is to get you to buy a product. In the three ads in this unit, the product is a "dream." Most of us would like to have these dreams come true in our own lives.

Work in groups. Discuss the "dream" that each ad is selling. Fill in the chart below. Then answer the questions that follow.

Ads	Dreams
Ad 1: New York State Lottery	
Ad 2: Okemo Ski Resort	
Ad 3: Cupid.com	

1. Which dream has the best chance of coming true, in your opinion?

2. Which dream would you "buy"? Why?

3. Which ad is the most effective for selling the dream?

B Analysis

Many popular ads are successful because they include humor. The best advertising gets our attention by making us laugh. There are different ways to include humor. Sometimes the people in the ads make funny comments. Sometimes ads include a funny song. Sometimes sound effects or background noises add humor.

Ads also play with language in order to get our attention. Unusual words or phrases are sometimes used to add humor.

Work in groups. Listen to the three ads again while you look at the transcripts on pages 149–150. Are the following comments from the ads funny? Is the language playful? (Not all the examples in the list are humorous.) Choose the ones you think are humorous and put them into the correct column of the chart on page 15.

Sick pipe, dude. ***If you say so, dude.***

Millions that is . . . ***lots of zeros!***

performing their ***gravity-defying deeds of daring***

Well, you'll find ***Mr. Button . . . uh . . .***

~~It can happen, *ya hear*?~~

She ***picked the winning numbers***, and she ***won a ton of cash.***

I hope the next one's a little brighter.

That's the sound of people ***enjoying the best conditions in the East.***

sculpting that snow like the frosting on your Aunt Tilly's icebox cake

~~So, whatever Mother Nature *dishes out*~~

snow that's been ***neglected and disrespected***

Ads	Funny Comments	Playful Language
Ad 1: New York State Lottery	*"It can happen, ya hear?"* (This is funny because of the informal way the singer talks to us.)	
Ad 2: Okemo Ski Resort		*"So, whatever Mother Nature dishes out."* (This is playful because Mother Nature doesn't usually dish things out; people do.)
Ad 3: Cupid.com		

© Creation

Work with another student. Write an ad that "sells a dream." Consider effective techniques you might use to get listeners interested. Include humor if you can. Read your ad to the class, or record your ad and play it for the class.

Pet Advice

Why do people have pets? What can pets do for people?

In recent years, call-in radio shows have become more and more popular. People listen to the radio shows about health, love relationships, cooking, or pets to find out how to improve their lives. They call the radio station to ask a question and get advice from an expert.

In this unit, you will hear three calls.

LISTENING 1: A call from Leslie on *The Jon Katz Show*

LISTENING 2: A call from Jodi on the show *Pets with Sue Sternberg*

LISTENING 3: A call from Kathleen, also on *Pets with Sue Sternberg*

Jon Katz at home with his dogs.

Work in groups. Discuss your answers to the following questions.

1. Two-thirds (2/3) of American families own a dog. Why are dogs such popular pets?
2. Should people meet certain requirements to own a dog? If so, what are they?

Ⓐ Vocabulary Preview

Read the following sentences. Guess the meaning of the underlined words. Then match each word with a definition or synonym on page 18.

____ **1.** My two dogs are very different: One <u>barks</u> each time someone comes to the house; the other is always silent.

____ **2.** After many <u>complaints</u> from his neighbors, Joe finally decided to give his dog away.

____ **3.** Erica cannot leave her puppy <u>loose</u> in the house, or it will chew the furniture!

____ **4.** I can only work at the computer for two hours <u>at a stretch</u> before I need to take a break.

____ **5.** Our puppy was <u>crated</u> for six months when we first got it. She actually liked it and felt safe in her own little home.

____ **6.** Open the windows! I don't think there's enough <u>ventilation</u> in here.

___ **7.** That man is so <u>cruel</u> to his dog. He leaves her locked up all day with no food or water!

___ **8.** I only read my personal e-mail on my office computer when I'm <u>off the clock</u>. I never take time away from work.

___ **9.** I used to be bothered by the traffic noise outside my window, but after three years I've developed a <u>desensitization</u>.

a. process that makes someone react less strongly to something

b. free to move around

c. fresh air in a room

d. without stopping

e. not being paid to work

f. put in a large box or cage

g. deliberately hurting people or animals or making them feel unhappy

h. makes the sound that a dog makes

i. statements in which you say you are annoyed or unhappy about something

Ⓑ Listening for the Main Ideas

Listen to the call. Answer the following questions. Discuss your answers with a partner.

1. What is Leslie's problem?
2. What is Jon's advice?

Ⓒ Listening for Details

Read the following questions. Listen to the call again. Circle the best answer for each question. Compare your answers with those of another student.

1. How old is Leslie's beagle?
a. $5\frac{1}{2}$ years   **b.** 2 years

2. How many apartments are there in Leslie's apartment house?
a. 2   **b.** 4

3. How long will Leslie leave his dog alone in the apartment?
a. only 1 to 2 hours   **b.** anywhere from 1 to 5 hours

4. What does Jon recommend putting in the crate?
a. a bone and water   **b.** a towel or blanket

5. Why do people think it's cruel to put a dog in a crate?

    a. because it would be cruel to put humans in one   **b.** because dogs don't need to be in a closed space

6. What is "doggie Zen"?

    a. a time for dogs to relax   **b.** a time for dogs to work hard

7. What does Jon think is the best thing to do?

    a. the desensitization to sound technique   **b.** the crate technique

8. Why can't Leslie ask his second question?

    a. because the show is over   **b.** because another call is coming in

D Listening for Inference

Sometimes people say what they think we want to hear. Other times their answers are more honest.

Listen to the excerpt from the call-in show. Listen to Leslie's response to Jon's question. Then answer the question. Discuss your answer with a partner.

How many hours do you think Leslie typically leaves his dog alone?

    a. 1 hour

    b. 2 hours

    c. 4 to 5 hours

E Discussion

Work in groups. Discuss your answers to the following questions.

1. Do you think it is a good idea to leave a dog in a crate for several hours? Why or why not?

2. Why do you think Jon tells his dog "You're a great dog. You're working very hard," when he puts his dog in the crate? What is he saying about his dog?

F Looking at Language

Function: Asking for Advice / Information

1. *Read the excerpt from the call as you listen to it. What is the purpose of the highlighted phrase? What is Leslie asking? Can you think of another way to say this?*

> Uh, I have a . . . about five-and-a-half-year-old beagle . . . I've had since he was two. I just recently moved like the beginning of February. I live in an apartment house with four apartments, and when he's left alone, he'll bark. Um . . . I don't know whether he did this where I used to live before . . . I never got any complaints. Um . . . **I just wondered if there's anything I could do.**

In the previous excerpt, Leslie is asking Jon for advice. He wants to know whether he can do something to stop his dog's barking. He is asking for suggestions.

When we ask for advice or information, there are certain phrases we use. Notice that some of these phrases introduce a question; they are followed by a question mark (?). Other phrases introduce a statement. These statements show something that the speaker doesn't know, but they are not presented as a question; they are followed by a period (.). Notice that the word order in these statements is *not* inverted question formation. In the previous excerpt, the caller says:

Um . . . I just wondered if <u>there's anything I could do.</u>
    (subject + verb +   complement)

If this were expressed as a question, inverted word order would be used:

Um . . . <u>Is there anything I could do?</u>
    (verb + subject + complement)

Here are some common phrases that introduce statements or questions that ask for advice:

I'd like to know . . .
I'm interested in . . .
I wonder if you could tell me . . .
Could you tell me . . . ?
Do you know . . . ?
Could I ask . . . ?
Do you happen to know . . . ?
This may sound like a dumb question, but I'd like to know . . .
Something else I'd like to know is . . .

2. *Read the following mini-dialogues. Complete speaker A's part with a phrase from the list above. Check the punctuation for speaker A. Is it a question or a statement? Then complete speaker B's part with a phrase from the list on page 21. Finally, role-play the mini-dialogues with a partner. Then change roles.*

1. **A:** _____ why my dog has been drinking so much water all day?

   B: _____

2. **A:** _____ why my cat hides under the bed when people come over to my house?

   B: _____

3. **A:** _____ how to stop my puppy from eating my shoes?

   B: _____

4. **A:** _____ if I can give my dog leftovers from our dinner.

   B: _____

5. A: _____ when it's OK to separate kittens from their mother?

B: _____

6. A: _____ what to do when my dog jumps on people.

B: _____

- Cats are sometimes antisocial animals. This is not unusual behavior.
- Keep him on a short leash each time someone comes to visit you.
- Most human food is OK for dogs, but don't give him any onions.
- Summer is here, so the hotter it gets, the more water he needs.
- They should be at least eight weeks old before you give them away.
- You need to have enough toys for him because puppies need to chew.

LISTENING 2 "DOG EATS ANYTHING" WITH SUE STERNBERG

Work in groups. Discuss your answers to the following questions.

1. What kinds of behavior problems do dogs sometimes have?
2. What can people do if their dog has a behavior problem?

Ⓐ Vocabulary Preview

Read the definitions of the following words and phrases. Then complete the sentences with the best word or phrase.

harmful:	likely to cause damage or hurt someone
outgrow:	no longer enjoy something you used to enjoy when you were younger
screw:	
intestines:	the long tubes that take food from your stomach out of your body
bolt:	suddenly start to run very fast
grab:	take hold of something with a sudden movement
forbidden:	not allowed
puppy-proof:	made so as not to be harmed by puppies or to protect puppies against something
odds and ends:	various small things
isolated:	separated from other people

1. When I was growing up, our dogs and cats were _____ to come in the house. They were outdoor animals.

2. My puppy chews everything in the house. I certainly hope he will _____ this behavior soon!

3. Most dogs prefer being around people rather than being _____ in a separate space.

4. Gently feed the dog his bone, or he might _____ it out of your hand!

5. I need to pick up some _____ at the drugstore. Do you want to come with me?

6. We needed to _____ our home before bringing the new puppy home, so we picked up everything off the floor and bought him some dog toys to play with.

7. My father had problems with his _____ and had to go into the hospital.

8. Whenever the doorbell rang, our dog would _____ for the door to greet our guests.

9. Please take this _____ and put my picture frame back together.

10. I don't want to drink soda anymore because I know that it is _____ to my body.

Ⓑ Listening for the Main Ideas

Listen to the call. Answer the following questions. Discuss your answers with a partner.

1. What is Jodi's problem?

2. What three pieces of advice does Sue give the caller?

Ⓒ Listening for Details

Listen to the call again. Then cross out the answer that is NOT correct. Compare your answers with those of another student.

1. Jodi has had her pug _____.
  a. for three years   **b.** since she was   **c.** ever since she
                                six months old   was a puppy

2. Jodi's pug picks up _____.
  a. metal   **b.** plastic   **c.** only small things

3. If the children drop something, the dog will _____.
  a. bolt toward it   **b.** take off with it   **c.** leave it

4. The dog has _____.
  a. toys   **b.** bones   **c.** games

5. What gets the family involved in the dog's play is _____.
  a. her own toys   **b.** screws and   **c.** remote controls and
                             eyeglasses   plastic baggies

6. Sue suggests that the family _____.
  a. puppy-proof   **b.** pick up the dog   **c.** buy a series of new toys
      the house

7. If the dog picks up a forbidden item, _____.
  a. the family   **b.** the family should   **c.** the family should run
      should call her   stop watching   into the bathroom
      name and pet her   videos or working
                           on the computer

8. When the family comes out of the bathroom, the dog will _____.
  a. probably be   **b.** have dropped the   **c.** be wondering why
      chewing the item   item on the floor   everyone left

D Listening for Inference

Listen to the excerpts from the call-in show. For each excerpt, listen to Jodi's response to Sue. Listen to her tone of voice. How convinced does she sound? Circle the number that represents how "convinced" or "unconvinced" she seems to be. After each excerpt, discuss your answer with a partner.

Excerpt 1

unconvinced   convinced

←---→
      1   2   3   4   5

Excerpt 2

unconvinced   convinced

←---→
      1   2   3   4   5

Excerpt 3

unconvinced   convinced

←---→
      1   2   3   4   5

E Discussion

Work in groups. Discuss your answers to the following questions.

1. Jodi's dog eats anything. Sue says it's a way to get Jodi's attention. What else do pets do to get attention from humans?
2. Sue suggests the family leave the room when the dog picks up something he should not pick up. In your opinion, can we stop bad behaviors in pets (or children) by ignoring them?

F Looking at Language

Grammar: Compound Adjectives

1. *Read the excerpt from the call-in show. Look at the highlighted phrases. Why is the word **year** singular in the first example? Why is the word **months** plural in the second example?*

> *Jodi*: Hi. Thank you for taking my call. I have a . . . almost **three-year-old** pug, and . . . um . . . she eats twice a day. We got her when she was **six months old**, and ever since she's been a puppy, um . . . we try to keep things out of her reach that could be harmful to her, and we thought she'd outgrow it, but she . . . this morning I found her with a big, metal screw in her mouth, chasing her around the house to try and get it out . . .
> *Sue*: OK . . .

The highlighted phrases above are compound adjectives. When a compound adjective appears before the noun (three-year-old pug) as in the first example, it is hyphenated and the modifying noun (*year*) is singular. When a compound adjective appears after the noun (she was six months old), it is *not* hyphenated and the modifying noun (*months*) is plural.

2. Rewrite the sentences to use compound hyphenated adjectives. The first one has been done for you.

1. My dog ate a box of candy that weighed two pounds.

My dog ate a *two-pound box of candy.*

2. My pug weighs 10 pounds.

I have a _____

3. My dog is two feet tall.

I have a _____

4. Our puppy is six months old.

We have a _____

5. My dog will eat a screw that is two inches long!

My dog will eat a _____

6. I live in an apartment that has four rooms.

I live in a _____

7. You can leave your dog in the crate for a stretch of four hours.

You can leave your dog in the crate for a _____

8. My dog sleeps in a crate that is three feet tall.

My dog sleeps in a _____

9. My dog drinks out of a water bowl that holds two quarts.

My dog drinks out of a _____

10. Each day my dog likes to take a nap for two hours.

Each day my dog likes to take a _____

Work in groups. Discuss your answers to the following questions.

1. People sometimes ask, "Are you a cat person or a dog person?" Why do people assume that there is a difference between people who own dogs and people who own cats? Which pet would you prefer?
2. What kinds of problems do people sometimes have with cats?

Ⓐ Vocabulary Preview

Read the following letter. Guess the meaning of the underlined words. Then match each word with a definition or synonym from page 27.

> Dear Sue Sternberg,
>
> Ever since my childhood, my (**1**) <u>household</u> has been filled with cats! We always had at least five cats living in the house with us, and at times there were even ten or twelve of them if one of the cats had kittens. So, I know a lot about cats! However, I think I need your (**2**) <u>guidance</u> in solving a problem I'm having today with my two cats.
>
> I've been living with my cat, Buster, for two years. He is very (**3**) <u>antisocial</u> and stays under the bed most of the day, especially when people visit me. The other day, my sister went with me to the local (**4**) <u>shelter</u> to get another cat. I wanted Buster to have a playmate. I thought this would help him become more social. We saw a beautiful cat at the shelter. Tiger had been a (**5**) <u>stray</u> and had been picked up off the street just a few weeks earlier. As soon as we picked him up and (**6**) <u>stroked</u> his

soft coat, he purred and looked very happy. So, we brought Tiger home to live with me and Buster.

Tiger and Buster do not get along well. When I came home with the new cat, Buster came downstairs and tried to (**7**) <u>scratch</u> his eyes out! I keep the cats in different rooms, but Buster knows Tiger is in the house. He has been (**8**) <u>growling</u> at night, so I can't sleep.

Is this a problem of cat (**9**) <u>hierarchy</u>? Is Buster afraid of (**10**) <u>switching</u> his top-cat position with the new cat in the household? What can I do? Please help!

Sincerely yours,
Helene McGreevy

_____ **a.** animal that has no home

_____ **b.** all the people who live together in one house

_____ **c.** making deep angry sounds

_____ **d.** moved hands gently over

_____ **e.** helpful advice

_____ **f.** changing

_____ **g.** a system of organization in which people (or animals) have higher and lower ranks

_____ **h.** place where animals receive protection and care

_____ **i.** make a small cut in a surface with something sharp (like with a cat's claws)

_____ **j.** not comfortable being with people

B Listening for the Main Ideas

Listen to the call. Answer the following questions. Discuss your answers with a partner.

1. What is Kathleen's problem?
2. What is Sue's advice?

C Listening for Details

Read the following statements. Listen to the call again. Mark the statements T (true) or F (false). Compare your answers with those of another student.

_____ **1.** Kathleen has one kitten.

_____ **2.** Cat number 3 (the stray cat) needed a playmate.

_____ **3.** Cat number 1 and cat number 3 don't get along.

___ **4.** Kathleen wants to reintroduce the cats after she moves.

___ **5.** Cat number 3 is the only female cat.

___ **6.** Sue wants Kathleen to separate the cats completely.

___ **7.** Sue wants Kathleen to feed the cats together.

___ **8.** The cats should meet at a crack* in the door.   *small opening

___ **9.** Dog hierarchy is stronger than cat hierarchy.

___**10.** The cats should play together for ten minutes.

D Listening for Inference

Listen to the excerpt from the call-in show. Then answer the question below. Discuss your answer with a partner.

Sue changes her response to Kathleen. Which of the following best describes what Sue really thinks?

    a. She wouldn't switch the rooms.
    b. She doesn't care if the rooms are switched.
    c. She thinks the best thing is to switch the rooms.

E Discussion

Work in groups. Discuss your answers to the following questions.

    1. Are cats antisocial, in your opinion? Are they less social than dogs or other pets?
    2. Have you ever seen "hierarchy" with pets? Describe the situation. Which pet had more power? Which pet had less power? Why?

F Looking at Language

Pronunciation: Compound Nouns

1. *Read the excerpt from the call-in show as you listen to it. Which syllable in each of the highlighted words is stressed?*

> *Kathleen:* I have three cats who have been introduced to the **household** at different times, and cat number 1 has been around for about five years, from a shelter; cat number 2, who's still a kitten, joined our house in August of last year . . .
>
> *Sue:* OK.
>
> *Kathleen:* . . . and then cat number 3 just came around in January. Uh, he was a stray who needed a house, and so, and the kitten needed a **playmate**. . . so, it was one of those types of situations.

The highlighted words in the previous excerpt are compound nouns. Compound nouns are formed by combining two nouns and using them together to make one word. In pronouncing a compound noun, the first noun is more heavily stressed than the second one. It is also pronounced on a higher pitch.

hóusehold

pláymate

2. Read the following mini-dialogues. Use the compound nouns in the lists below to complete the sentences. (Note that some compound nouns are two words.) Then work in pairs to read the dialogues. Practice the correct stress.

bedroom	dog food	doorway
eyeballs	fireplace	lampshade
lightbulb	mailbox	mail carrier
toenails		

1. **A:** I can't believe you let your cat play in your face like that!

   B: I cut my cat's _____, so she can't scratch my _____ out!

2. **A:** How do you know that your dog barks while you're out of the house?

   B: The _____ said he hears my dog barking each time he walks up to my _____.

3. **A:** What happened in here?

   B: The kitten knocked over the lamp, tore the _____, and broke the _____!

4. **A:** Your dog looks very comfortable there . . . in front of the fire.

   B: Yes, every evening he finishes eating his _____ and lies in front of the _____ to get warm.

5. **A:** How can we keep the cats separated?

   B: Let's put the kitten in the _____ and close off the _____ to the next room.

Now change roles.

baseball	buttermilk	eyeglasses
firefighter	girlfriend	laptop
newspaper	seafood	sidewalk
windowsill		

6. **A:** I heard you couldn't get your cat down from a tree!

   B: That's right. The story was even printed in the _____.
   A _____ had to come and take her down with a ladder!

7. **A:** Why are you buying so many cans of tuna?

   B: My cat is a picky eater. She will only eat _____, and she
   will only drink _____!

8. **A:** Doesn't your cat ever go out of the house?

   B: No, she loves to sit on the _____ and watch people walk
   up and down the _____ all day.

9. **A:** Why is your son crying?

   B: My dog eats everything. The dog just chewed his _____,
   so he can't see, and he chewed his _____, so he can't
   practice for the game tonight!

10. **A:** What's the matter?

    B: I'm trying to type an e-mail to my _____, but my cat
    keeps jumping on my lap and walking over my _____.

WRAP UP

Ⓐ Synthesis

Call-in radio shows are popular because people call in to the shows with common
questions. Many listeners may have problems similar to the caller's problem.

*Work in groups. Consider the advice given for the three calls about pets. How
useful is the advice? How likely is it that the caller, other listeners, or you might
take the advice? In the chart on page 31, rate the advice for each call from 1 to 5,
with 5 being* **very likely** *and 1 being* **unlikely**. *Discuss your answers with other
students.*

	Call 1 (Dog Barks)	Call 2 (Dog Eats Anything)	Call 3 (Cat Hierarchy)
Will the caller follow the advice?			
Will listeners follow the advice?			
If you had a pet, would *you* follow the advice?			

B Analysis

Call-in radio shows are successful because the experts give concrete (clearly based on facts) advice to people. People can immediately use the advice to make changes in their lives. A good call-in radio show gives people very concrete suggestions for change.

Review the three calls from this unit. What concrete advice is offered to the caller? What can the caller do today to change his or her pet's behavior? Make a list of concrete suggestions. The first one has been done for you.

Call 1   *Put the dog in a covered crate while out.*

_____

Call 2   _____

_____

Call 3   _____

_____

C Creation

Design your own call-in radio show. Follow these steps.

1. Find someone in the class who can give good advice on a particular subject. (Consider pets, relationships with people, cooking, finding a place to live, sports, etc.)
2. Write questions for the particular subject that was chosen in step 1. Imagine that you will call in to a radio show with your question. (Use language from this unit.)
3. Conduct a call-in show. Class members present their problems and ask questions. The expert answers the question and gives concrete advice.

Boyhood Memories

What kinds of things do you remember from your childhood?

A monologue is a long period of talking by one person. People use monologues when they tell stories or remember important events from the past. A monologue is not a conversation with other people. (That's a dialogue.)

In this unit, you will hear three monologues in which men recall something important about their boyhood.

LISTENING 1: In "A Wonderful Life," David Greenberger retells a story from a conversation he had with Gene Weaver about Gene's favorite childhood toys.

LISTENING 2: In "A Death in the Family," Martin Jacobson tells a story to his granddaughter about the death of a family member during his boyhood.

LISTENING 3: Noah Adams, a reporter from National Public Radio, uses a monologue to tell his story, "Young Romance," a memory of an early love.

Work in groups. Discuss your answers to the following questions.

1. Did you have any favorite toys when you were a child? Describe the toys and why they were so special.

2. Did you ever make your own toys when you were a child?

Ⓐ Vocabulary Preview

Work in small groups. Match the words to the pictures. Write a letter on the lines. Use a dictionary only if necessary.

a.

b.

c.

d.

e.

f.

g.

h.

____ **1.** Airedale dog   ____ **5.** hinges

____ **2.** stagecoach   ____ **6.** chest of drawers

____ **3.** gadget   ____ **7.** quilt

____ **4.** yo-yo   ____ **8.** duplex house

B Listening for the Main Ideas

Listen to the monologue. Answer the following questions. Discuss your answers with a partner.

1. What toys did the man make when he was a boy?
2. What did the man enjoy most about his childhood?

C Listening for Details

1. *Read the following list of events. Listen to the first part of the monologue again. Number the events in the order in which they happened. Write a number from 1 to 6 next to each event. Compare your answers with those of another student.*

____ He made a yo-yo.

____ He let the yo-yo fly up and down.

____ He crawled up on top of the house.

____ He started making gadgets.

____ He saw the first yo-yos in 1927.

____ He found something in the garbage.

2. *Read the following statements. Listen to the second part of the monologue again. Mark the statements T (true) or F (false). Compare your answers with those of another student.*

____ 1. He got enough boys to pull his stagecoach.

____ 2. His stagecoach was as big as a chest of drawers.

____ 3. His family had an Airedale dog.

____ 4. The dog was beautiful.

____ 5. The dog rode the stagecoach with the boys.

____ 6. He had a dog after he was married.

____ 7. He wishes he had been a girl.

____ 8. The hinges on his stagecoach were made out of leather.

D Listening for Inference

Listen to the excerpts from the monologue. Then answer the questions. Discuss your answer with a partner.

1. What do you think of when you think about cowboys?
2. Why does the speaker refer to himself as a cowboy?
3. What is he suggesting about his personality in these comments?

E Discussion

Work in groups. Discuss your answers to the following questions.

1. The speaker says he "can remember those hinges and that stagecoach and that yo-yo." However, he says he "can't remember what happened yesterday." Why do you think this is so?
2. What kinds of memories do people usually keep as they grow older? Why?

F Looking at Language

Pronunciation: Thought Groups

1. *Read the excerpt from the monologue as you listen to it. Notice the grouped words. Why does the speaker pause in between each of these phrases? Why do you think the words of these phrases are grouped together?*

And I liked to make gadgets, I liked to make things, and I started out

around eight years old—well, I started out at three years old I guess,

four years old, making a tent in the living room out of quilts.

In the above excerpt, the speaker pauses in between each phrase. The phrases are thought groups, meaningful groups of words or phrases pronounced together. Pausing is especially important in a monologue. Your listeners will understand you more easily if you break up your ideas into thought groups. It helps your listeners organize the meaning of your sentences.

If you pause between different groups of words, you can change the meaning of a sentence. Listen to how different thought groups can affect the meaning of this sentence.

John had wonderful boyhood memories of his grandfather.

John had wonderful boyhood memories of his grand father.

(In the first sentence, John's memories are of the father of one of his parents. In the second sentence, his memories are of his father, who was a great man.)

Philip carefully closed the lid to his old toy chest.

Philip carefully closed the lid to his old toy chest.

(In the first sentence, it is not an actual chest, but a toy. In the second sentence, it is a chest where he keeps his toys.)

2. Listen to the following pairs of sentences in the left column. Match each sentence in the left column with its meaning in the right column. Listen to how the thought groups affect the meaning.

Sentence	Meaning
1. a. His grandfather was an old woodworker.	**c.** His grandfather was old.
b. His grandfather was an old wood worker.	**d.** His grandfather worked with old wood.
2. a. That's the new cowboy.	**c.** That's his family name.
b. That's the Nucow boy.	**d.** There are two kinds of cowboys. That one is the new one.
3. a. The roof was a pretty high place to be on.	**c.** It was pretty, and high.
b. The roof was a pretty, high place to be on.	**d.** It was quite high.
4. a. The stagecoach had leather hinges, and doors.	**c.** The hinges were leather.
b. The stagecoach had leather hinges and doors.	**d.** Both the hinges and doors were leather.
5. a. Gene said, "David liked being a boy."	**c.** David liked being a boy.
b. "Gene," said David, "liked being a boy."	**d.** Gene liked being a boy.
6. a. His favorite toys were a stagecoach and yo-yo.	**c.** He had three favorite toys.
b. His favorite toys were a stage, coach, and yo-yo.	**d.** He had two favorite toys.

3. Read the sentences in Exercise 2 with a partner. Student A reads either sentence a or sentence b. Student B listens and reads the correct meaning, c or d. Then switch roles.

Work in groups. Discuss your answer to the following question.

How can the death of a child affect a family—the parents, sisters, or brothers?

A **Vocabulary Preview**

Read the following sentences. Guess the meaning of the underlined words. Then match each word with the letter of a definition or synonym from below.

____ **1.** During the war, the family experienced much <u>tragedy</u>: the loss of a son, the loss of their home, and family illness.

____ **2.** The most <u>devastating</u> thing for parents is the death of a child.

____ **3.** Eric's dad is so <u>bombastic</u>; you can never be sure if he's telling the truth!

____ **4.** Amy spent several days in the hospital after having a <u>nervous breakdown</u>.

____ **5.** Don't tell Lydia that you think she might not get the job. She is so <u>fragile</u>, that I'm afraid it will only make her situation worse!

____ **6.** We thought the teacher was <u>ridiculous</u> when she asked parents to spend three hours each night doing homework with their children!

____ **7.** Now that Dan is on the soccer team, he has much more <u>self-confidence</u>.

a. easily hurt
b. very sad experience
c. using long words that sound important but have no real meaning
d. a mental illness in which someone becomes extremely anxious and tired and cannot live and work normally
e. silly or unreasonable
f. feeling that you can do things well
g. badly damaging or destroying

B Listening for the Main Ideas

Listen to the monologue. Answer the following question. Discuss your answer with a partner.

How did the death of Martin's brother affect the family?

    a. The father behaved strangely, but the mother didn't.

    b. The mother behaved strangely, but the father didn't.

    c. Both the mother and father behaved strangely.

C Listening for Details

Read the following sentences. Listen to the monologue again. Fill in the missing information. Compare your answers with those of another student.

1. Martin's brother died at the age of _____, when Martin was around _____ years old.

2. The most devastating thing that can happen to a family is to _____.

3. Martin's father was not _____; he was a quiet guy.

4. When he _____, he went into a _____.

5. Instead of going to work, he was _____ with the kids.

6. His mother insisted on _____ in the morning to go to school.

7. He lost a lot of his _____ because his mother dressed him when he was ten or twelve.

8. Martin's mother couldn't _____ him or put her _____ around him.

D Listening for Inference

Listen to the excerpts from the monologue. Answer the questions. Discuss your answers with a partner.

Excerpt 1

How did Martin feel?

    a. hurt

    b. embarrassed

    c. angry

Excerpt 2

How did Martin feel?

    a. hurt
    b. embarrassed
    c. angry

Ⓔ Discussion

Work in groups. Discuss your answers to the following questions.

   1. Why do you think Martin's father played games with the kids? Why do you think his mother insisted on dressing Martin in the morning?

   2. Martin describes his parents' behaviors after losing their son. How do you think Martin felt after the death of his brother? What did he think about?

Ⓕ Looking at Language

Function: Interrupting

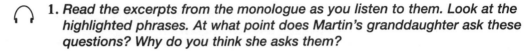

   1. *Read the excerpts from the monologue as you listen to them. Look at the highlighted phrases. At what point does Martin's granddaughter ask these questions? Why do you think she asks them?*

It was the most devastating thing that can happen to a family . . . to lose a child. (**And his name was?**) Sydney. It threw a pall over the house forever.

It was like, how can you be happy? Sydney is . . . Sydney died. (**And died of?**) Spinal meningitis.

Now I'd be sitting on a kitchen table, and she'd be putting my socks and shoes on, and I'd say, "Ma, let me do this." (**And how old were you?**) I was probably around 10 . . . 12. I mean, you don't do that.

In the above excerpts, Martin's granddaughter interrupts Martin as he tells his story. Notice that she does not interrupt him in the middle of a sentence. She waits until he has finished a sentence. Then she interrupts with a question. She wants to know some details during his monologue. When listening to our family members or friends, we often interrupt this way.

However, when we have more formal conversations, we may need to interrupt politely. For example, if you are listening to a teacher or someone you do not know very well, you might want to interrupt politely to ask a question.

Here are some useful phrases for interrupting politely:

Sorry, but . . .

Sorry to interrupt, but . . .

Excuse me for interrupting, but . . .

Can I say something here?

I'd like to comment on that.

I'd just like to say that . . .

I'd like to add something . . .

May I say/ask something?

2. Work in pairs. Student A tells a short story about something that happened to his or her family during childhood. Student B listens, interrupting politely from time to time to ask questions. Then switch roles.

LISTENING 3 "YOUNG ROMANCE" BY NOAH ADAMS

Work in groups. Discuss your answers to the following questions.

Valentine's Day is celebrated each year on February 14. On this day, people give cards, candy, or flowers to people they love. Is Valentine's Day celebrated in your culture? If so, what do people do?

A Vocabulary Preview

Read the definitions of the following words and phrases. Then complete the sentences with the best word or phrase.

muffled up:	covered in warm clothing
homemade:	made at home rather than bought in a store
exchange:	the act of giving someone one thing and receiving something from that person at the same time
assumed:	thought of something as true
lost his nerve:	stopped being confident
tore it up:	destroyed it by tearing it into small pieces
incriminating:	showing guilt
storm drain:	place where excess water runs off the street when it rains
regret:	to feel sorry about something you have done and wish you had not done it

1. It had rained a lot the day before, and the street was flooded because there was no _____.

2. Tom was planning to tell Jane that he loved her, but he didn't have much self-confidence and _____.

3. Our family lived in northern Minnesota, so in winter we always went to school _____ in hats, scarves, and mittens.

4. Josh's family always celebrated the holidays with a(n) _____ of gifts. Each family member brought a gift for one other member.

5. When my sister received the love letter from the new boy in her class, she _____ and threw it away. She felt so embarrassed.

6. My mother always served us her _____ fruit jelly for breakfast. She never bought jams or jellies in a store.

7. The information in that letter is very _____; the court will find him guilty of the crime.

8. The teacher _____ that his students had studied for the test because they all got good grades on it.

9. Although I think my father always knew that I loved him, I _____ the fact that I never told him.

B Listening for the Main Ideas

Listen to the monologue. Answer the following questions. Discuss your answers with a partner.

1. What did the kids in Noah's class do on Valentine's Day?
   a. They exchanged valentines with each other.
   b. They gave a valentine to the one they loved.
   c. They gave valentines to their teacher.

2. What does Noah regret?
   a. his feelings about Martha Jane
   b. telling others how he felt about them
   c. unsent valentines

C Listening for Details

Listen to the monologue again. Then cross out the answer that is NOT correct. Compare your answers with those of another student.

1. Noah's story takes place _____.
   a. on the 14th of February   b. three years ago   c. 30 years ago

2. The kids _____.
   a. walked to school   b. wore black rubber   c. were six years old
      in the snow   buckle-up-the-front boots

3. They had made valentines for _____.
   a. everyone in the class   b. the kids they liked   c. only some kids

4. Some of the kids in the back _____.
   a. got no valentines at all   b. were unloved   c. were loved

5. After school, Noah _____.
   a. went downtown   b. bought a card   c. met Martha Jane
      to the drugstore   for Martha Jane   in the park

6. Noah took the valentine card and _____.
   a. wrote his feelings   b. slipped it into Martha   c. tore it up and
      about Martha Jane on it   Jane's mailbox   threw it away

D Listening for Inference

Read the following statements. Listen to the monologue again. Mark the statements T (true) or F (false). Discuss your answers with a partner.

____ 1. Noah feels like his story about the sixth-grade classroom happened not so long ago.

____ **2.** Noah accepted the fact that not all kids got valentines.

____ **3.** Noah felt sorry for the kids in the back.

____ **4.** Noah was embarrassed by his valentine to Martha Jane.

____ **5.** Noah doesn't think we should express our love.

E **Discussion**

Work in groups. Discuss your answers to the following questions.

1. What do you think of Noah's story? Would you have done what he did?
2. Did you ever have a secret love when you were a child? Did you ever tell that person about your feelings? Why or why not?

F **Looking at Language**

Grammar: *Would* for Repeated Action in the Past

1. *Read the excerpt from the monologue as you listen to it. Listen for the use of* would *in the story. What does* would *mean in these examples?*

   In the morning, everybody **would** put their valentines in a box up
   on the teacher's desk, and then after lunch, all the valentines **would**
   be passed out. Everyone **would** start counting. Some kids **would**
   get valentines from almost everybody else in the class.

   > In this excerpt, Noah is describing repeated actions in the past. The verbs
   > all use *would* because they describe an action that was routine, habitual,
   > or characteristic of the class activities on Valentine's Day in his school. We
   > use this form when we tell stories about repeated past actions. To form the
   > habitual past with *would*, we use *would* + base verb.

2. *Work in pairs. Tell your partner about a typical event in your childhood. (It could
   be about school activities, family holidays, or things you did with friends.) Use
   the* would *verb form to express regularly repeated events in your life. Think
   about the following questions:*

   - Where would you go?
   - Who would go with you?
   - What would you do?
   - When would you do it?
   - How often would you do it?

WRAP UP

A **Synthesis**

In Listenings 1, 2, and 3, the men think back on their boyhoods. Each boyhood
memory brings up different emotions, different feelings.

1. *Work in pairs. Review the transcripts on pages 153–155. Discuss which feelings are expressed in each monologue. Give examples from the monologue to support your choices. Draw lines to connect the feelings to each monologue.*

embarrassed   *hurt*

proud   Listening 1   *nervous*
            "A Wonderful Life"

            Listening 2
         "A Death in the Family"

            Listening 3
excited   "Young Romance"   *regretful*

      sad   *shy*

2. *Which feelings best describe your childhood memories? Why? Give examples. Share your thoughts with the class.*

B Analysis

It is not easy to hold the attention of a listener for a long period of time. It is important to keep a listener's interest. One way to do this is to give many vivid details. The listener needs to "see" what is happening in your story. In each of the monologues, the speaker gives vivid details to help the listener "see" his story. We relive the speaker's boyhood memory with him.

Listen as you read the following excerpt of Gene's boyhood memory from David's monologue. The highlighted phrase is very descriptive, very vivid. We can almost see this young boy going through the garbage to find what he needs to make his toy. Where else does the speaker help us "see a picture" in his story? Underline the vivid details. Discuss your ideas with the class.

> "I was **rummaging around in the garbage** one day, and I found a thing that you put in rugs, you know, to roll them, like a core, and on the end there they had a flange on it. And I got two of those. And I made me a yo-yo, but it was a big yo-yo, a couple feet around. And of course, the only way you could use it, I figured I'd have to crawl up on top of the house, and that's what I did. I crawled up on the house and that was pretty dangerous because, when you let that yo-yo down, by the time it goes down to the ground and comes back up, it's movin'! I mean, it's really flyin' and there's some weight to it. Well that's one of the things."

C Creation

1. *Write a short monologue of a childhood memory. Use vivid details to involve your listener. Use language from the Looking at Language sections in this unit.*

2. *Work in pairs. Student A reads his or her monologue. Student B should interrupt politely to ask questions as Student A reads. Change roles so that each student reads his or her monologue.*

4 Safety

Genre: *GOVERNMENT MESSAGES*

Government officials speak to reporters about mad cow disease, a deadly disease of cows that affects the central nervous system. The government had recalled 10,000 pounds of beef.

What safety concerns do you have in your daily life?

The United States government sometimes gives out different kinds of information on the radio or on TV. One type of information might be a warning about a certain product. Other information might be advice about how to avoid dangerous situations.

In this unit, you will hear three U.S. government messages. Each one focuses on a different way we can live more safely.

LISTENING 1: A warning from the Federal Trade Commission, a U.S. government organization which makes sure that the nation's businesses can compete fairly

LISTENING 2: A message from the Department of Homeland Security, a U.S. government organization concerned with protecting the American homeland and the safety of American citizens

LISTENING 3: An announcement from the National Interagency Fire Center, a government organization that fights wildfires

Work in groups. Discuss your answers to the following questions.

1. Do you use the Internet often? Do you ever see things on the Internet that you would prefer not to see? If so, explain.

2. Should children be able to use the Internet freely? Should parents be able to control their children's use of the Internet? If so, how can they control it?

Ⓐ Vocabulary Preview

Read the following paragraphs. Guess the meaning of the underlined words. Then match the number of each word with a definition or synonym from page 47.

Brittany had to ask her parents for (**1**) <u>permission</u> to use the family computer. They worried about her (**2**) <u>privacy</u>. They did not want her to give out her personal information to websites. Brittany's parents were also concerned about the amount of time she spent on the Internet. She usually had two to three hours of homework each night, so (**3**) <u>surfing</u> the web was not possible.

To (**4**) <u>protect</u> her, Brittany's parents had not given her the (**5**) <u>password</u> to get online. Each time she wanted to use the computer, she had to ask her father to (**6**) <u>log on to</u> her favorite website. This became a bit of a problem for her father because Brittany had five brothers and sisters. They all had to wait their (**7**) <u>turn</u> to use the computer!

_____ **a.** time when it is your chance to do something

_____ **b.** prevent someone from being harmed

_____ **c.** secret word or phrase

_____ **d.** state of being able to keep your own affairs secret

_____ **e.** act of allowing someone to do something

_____ **f.** start using a computer by typing a special word

_____ **g.** looking quickly through information on the Internet

B Listening for the Main Ideas

Listen to the government message. Answer the following question. Discuss your answer with a partner.

Which of the following best expresses the main idea?

    a. The mother doesn't want her daughter to go online.

    b. The mother wants to see if her daughter's privacy is protected on a website.

    c. The mother wants her daughter to spend less time surfing online.

C Listening for Details

Read the following statements. Listen to the government message again. Mark the statements T (true) or F (false). Compare your answers with those of another student.

_____ **1.** It's the daughter's turn to go online.

_____ **2.** The mother asks her daughter to log on to her favorite website.

_____ **3.** The daughter's website has information about privacy on it.

_____ **4.** Children's e-mail addresses are *not* private information.

_____ **5.** The daughter can give information about herself without her parents' permission.

_____ **6.** The law that protects children while online is new.

_____ **7.** The daughter wants her mother to give her more time to surf online.

_____ **8.** The Federal Trade Commission gives information online.

D Listening for Inference

Read the following statements. Listen to the excerpts. Mark the statements A (agree) or D (disagree). Discuss your answers with a partner.

Excerpt 1

_____ The daughter probably doesn't know what "privacy" means.

Excerpt 2

_____ The mother will probably give her daughter more time to surf online.

E Discussion

Work in groups. Discuss your answers to the following questions.

1. In your opinion, should parents worry about their children going online? Why or why not?
2. Do you think our privacy can be protected on the Internet? Why or why not?

F Looking at Language

Pronunciation: *Can* and *Can't*

1. *Read the excerpt from the government message as you listen to it. Focus on the highlighted words. How is the pronunciation of these two words different? Which word is stressed? Which one is not stressed?*

> See, this part of the website says they **can't** ask you to give information about yourself without your parents' permission. This way, you **can** check with me before you give a website any information.

It is sometimes difficult to hear the difference between *can* and *can't*. There is a difference in stress and vowel sound. *Can't* is stressed and *can* is usually not stressed. The vowel sound in *can't* is /æ/, like in the word *man*. The vowel sound in *can* is usually /ə/, as in the end of the word *chicken*. In addition, native English speakers don't usually pronounce the *t* in *can't*.

It is important to hear these differences in order to know whether a speaker is making a positive or negative statement. It is equally important that you pronounce the two words differently so that listeners know your meaning.

---

2. *Listen to the following sentences. Circle* **can** *or* **can't***. Compare your answers with those of another student.*

1. She *can / can't* get online right now.

2. I *can / can't* find that website for you.

3. She *can / can't* give her personal information.

4. Those websites *can / can't* ask me for personal information.

5. She *can / can't* spend more time online than her brother.

6. You *can / can't* call the Federal Trade Commission today.

3. *Work in pairs. Practice the pronunciation of* **can** *and* **can't.** *Student A reads each sentence, using either* **can** *or* **can't.** *Student B responds with either* "Really, how?" *or* "Really, why not?" *Student A responds with an explanation. Then change roles.*

EXAMPLE
A: I *can* find that website for you.
B: Really, how?
A: It's easy; just log on to this address.

1. I *can / can't* go online whenever I want.

2. I *can / can't* shop online easily.

3. I *can / can't* get good information on the Internet.

4. I *can / can't* communicate easily with friends online.

5. I *can / can't* spend hours surfing online.

6. I *can / can't* live without a computer.

| LISTENING 2 | A MESSAGE FROM THE DEPARTMENT OF HOMELAND SECURITY |

Work in groups. Discuss your answers to the following questions.

Have you changed the way you live in recent years for reasons of safety? What kinds of things do you do?

A Vocabulary Preview

Read the definitions of the following words and phrases. Then complete the sentences with the best word or phrase.

beyond (one's) control:	unable to make someone or something do what you want
have a plan in place:	have a set of actions ready for a possible future event
emergencies:	unexpected, dangerous situations that you must deal with immediately
peace of mind:	without worries
in the event:	used to tell people what they should do or what will happen if something else happens
common sense:	the ability to behave in a sensible way and make practical decisions
calm:	relaxed; not angry or upset

1. Even though he is very intelligent, Jerry doesn't have much _____ in his daily life and often makes bad choices.

2. It gives me _____ to know my children can reach me on my cell phone at any time of day.

3. The teachers in the school were told what to do _____ of a fire.

4. If there are any natural disasters or other _____, the radio will report them to the public twenty-four hours a day.

5. Even when everyone in my house argued and got upset, my mother always remained very _____.

6. You can prepare for hurricanes and floods, but certain events are _____.

7. We should _____ in case my parents' flight is canceled.

B Listening for the Main Ideas

Listen to the government message. Answer the following question. Discuss your answer with a partner.

What advice does the message give?

    a. Stay with your family.

    b. Buy the right food.

    c. Have a communication plan.

ⓒ Listening for Details

Read the following sentences. Listen to the government message again. Find and correct the errors in each sentence. The first one has been done for you.

1. You need to have a plan with your ~~neighbors~~. *family members*

2. This message was recorded in Washington, D.C.

3. One of the most important things is to have an escape plan.

4. You need enough blankets in your home if you're going to stay there a while.

5. There are things people can do to help themselves, their family members, and their friends.

6. The important thing is to use common sense and act quickly.

7. You can call for an inexpensive brochure.

ⓓ Listening for Inference

Listen to the excerpt from the government message. Write your answers to the following questions. Discuss your answers with a partner.

1. This message is from the U.S. Department of Homeland Security. What kind of emergency do you think this message is talking about?
2. What can people do to have some sort of communication plan in place? What do you think the message is suggesting we do?

ⓔ Discussion

Work in groups. Discuss your answers to the following questions.

1. How do you react to this government safety message? Does it help you? Does it make you feel more afraid?
2. Have you heard messages like this where you live? What do they say?

ⓕ Looking at Language

Function: Emphasizing a Point

1. *Read the last part of the government safety message as you listen to it. Notice the highlighted phrase. What function or purpose does it serve in this message?*

   We just want to have people know that there are things they can do to help themselves, to help their family members, to help their neighbors in the event something happens. **And the important thing is** to use common sense, to remain calm.

When speakers want to emphasize a point, they use certain phrases to show that something is important. In this excerpt, "And the important thing is" tells listeners that the information the speaker is going to say is important. It is a signal that we should listen more carefully. The following phrases emphasize a point:

> *And the important thing is . . .*
> *What's important here is that . . .*
> *The point is that . . .*
> *Don't forget that . . .*
> *I'd like to stress that . . .*
> *The thing we need to look at is . . .*
> *So, the real question is . . .*
> *The fact of the matter is . . .*

2. *Read the following situations. Work in pairs. For each of the three situations, write out conversations (six to eight lines) between the two people in their state of emergency. The two people should disagree on the best way to deal with the emergency situation. Use two or three phrases from the preceding list as well as new vocabulary. Practice your conversations. Then act out your conversations for the class.*

Situation 1

Natalie, Ted, and their two small children are on vacation at the beach. Yesterday they heard on the news that a dangerous hurricane was moving up the coast from the south. It is predicted that the hurricane will hit the small town where Natalie and Ted are staying sometime after midnight.

Most of the vacationing tourists have packed up their cars and are heading home. The roads have begun filling up with cars; they are moving very, very slowly. The worst thing is that, for Natalie and Ted, driving home means driving *into* the storm. On the radio, they are advising people to stay where they are and prepare for the storm.

Natalie and Ted must decide what to do. Ted says they should stay where they are; he believes they will be safe. Natalie is afraid of being in the storm and afraid of the effects it might bring: Flooding? Loss of electricity? She wants to leave.

Natalie: Let's pack the car and drive home now. Tomorrow this place will be in a state of emergency!

Ted: Well, OK, if you want to. But, *don't forget that* we'll be driving into the storm. I think we should stay!

Situation 2

Maria and her teenage son, Alex, have rented a beach house for the weekend. On their first day at the beach, a lifeguard explains to them that sharks had been spotted in the ocean just two weeks earlier. The beaches were closed for a few days. However, the beaches are now open, and people are swimming in the ocean.

Maria has heard news stories that more and more sharks have been approaching beaches. There has been an increase in the number of sharks attacking humans in recent years. People have lost arms and legs. One man even died. She tells Alex that she doesn't want him to swim in the water. She is very worried.

Alex feels that there is little or no chance of any danger of sharks. He tells his mother that they can't live being afraid of unlikely events. He points to all the people swimming happily in the ocean and tells his mother he's going in!

Situation 3

Josh and Andrew are college roommates. They will graduate from college in two days and have planned a big barbecue at their apartment to celebrate their graduation. They have invited 50 friends. Josh bought the meat for the hamburgers, and Andrew took care of buying chips and drinks.

Today there was a news story that someone in a nearby state was infected with mad cow disease, a disease that eats holes in the brains of cattle. If people eat the beef from these cows, they, too, become infected. Josh wants to throw away the meat he bought. He knows about the eighty people in Britain that have already died from this disease. He is worried that the meat he bought could be contaminated. He does not want to risk infecting the guests at his party.

Andrew says there is no chance that their meat is infected. He does not believe that the store where they shop could have such meat. He does not want to throw away perfectly good beef. Besides, it was very expensive, and they cannot afford to pay for any more food for the party.

Work in groups. Discuss your answer to the following question.

Wildfires can be a big problem, especially in dry places. These are fires that move quickly and are out of control. What can people do to avoid them?

A Vocabulary Preview

Read the following sentences. Guess the meaning of the underlined words. Then match each word with the letter of a definition or synonym from page 55.

_____ **1.** Mara and Lucy got lost while mountain climbing. Luckily, they were able to build a <u>campfire</u> to keep warm until their friends found them the next day.

_____ **2.** Karen found a great place to live, with beautiful trees, mountains, and rivers <u>surrounding</u> her home.

_____ **3.** Don't light a match near that bottle because it contains <u>flammable</u> material.

_____ **4.** Small children should never be left home <u>unattended</u>.

_____ **5.** Don't stand close to a fire. <u>Sparks</u> could fly out and harm you.

_____ **6.** It was a hot summer day, but a small ocean <u>breeze</u> made us feel cool.

_____ **7.** The fire began to go out, but after we <u>fanned the flames</u>, it started burning again.

_____ **8.** You must completely <u>drown</u> the fire with water when you are finished cooking on an open fire.

_____ **9.** Her coffee was too hot to drink, so she <u>stirred</u> some more milk in it to cool it off.

_____ **10.** We did not know whether or not it would rain, but we decided to <u>play it safe</u> and bring our things inside.

    a. all around

    b. left alone without being watched

    c. got a fire to burn by moving air around

    d. very small flashes of fire coming from a larger fire

    e. avoid taking any risks

    f. a small outdoor fire used for cooking or warmth

    g. easy to burn

    h. light gentle wind

    i. mixed around

    j. completely cover something with liquid

B Listening for the Main Ideas

Listen to the government message. Answer the following question. Discuss your answer with a partner.

What advice does the message give?

    a. Don't build campfires in wild lands.
    b. Be responsible when making fires.
    c. Only cook indoors, not outdoors.

C Listening for Details

Listen to the advice from the government message again. Fill in the missing words or phrases. All of them are from Section A.

Remember: Play it safe with campfires and outdoor cooking. Keep
(**1**) _____ small and clear the (**2**) _____ area
of (**3**) _____ material. Never leave your fire
(**4**) _____, and keep water nearby. Remember:
(**5**) _____ fly! Even a small (**6**) _____ can
(**7**) _____ _____ _____. When
it's time to go, (**8**) _____ fires with water and
(**9**) _____ in some dirt.

D Listening for Inference

A pun is a playful, funny use of language. Many words and phrases have two meanings in English. For example, notice the double meaning in the following sentence:

Do you know why it's easy for a hunter to find a leopard? Because a leopard is always **spotted**.

    spotted = with spots   spotted = seen or noticed

Listen to the introduction to the government message again. A pun is used to introduce it.

Try to explain the two possible meanings of **hot** *in the opening sentence. Discuss your ideas with another student.*

Here's a **hot topic** about our wild lands and living with the natural role of fire.

E Discussion

Work in groups. Discuss your answers to the following questions.

1. Wildfires have become a bigger and bigger problem around the world. Why do you think this is true?
2. What natural disasters do you worry about? Does your government help people to prepare for them in any way?

F Looking at Language

Grammar: Imperative Mood

1. *Read this excerpt from the government safety message. Notice the highlighted verbs in each sentence. What form of the verb is used in each case? Why does the speaker use this verb form?*

> If this sounds like you, **remember: Play** it safe with campfires and outdoor cooking. **Keep** campfires small and **clear** the surrounding area of flammable material. **Never leave** your fire unattended, and **keep** water nearby. **Remember:** Sparks fly! Even a small breeze can fan the flames. When it's time to go, **drown** fires with water and **stir** in some dirt. With a little campfire care, your spot will be there next time, too.

The imperative mood is often used to give strong advice or suggestions. It is also used to give orders or commands. Government messages often use the imperative mood to get people's attention. The message is simple, strong, and clear.

To form the imperative mood, omit the subject and use the base form of the verb. (The omitted subject of the verb is *you.*)

> EXAMPLE
> <u>Keep</u> campfires small and <u>clear</u> the surrounding area of flammable material.

To form the negative imperative mood, put *don't* or *never* before the verb.

> EXAMPLE
> <u>Don't leave</u> your fire unattended.
> <u>Never leave</u> your fire unattended.

---

2. *Work in two groups, A and B. Each group stands in a line so that Group A faces Group B. Follow the directions on page 57. Then switch roles.*

Group A

- Each student chooses a different problem from the problems list. Tell a student facing you in Group B your problem. Ask for advice.
- After Student B has made a strong suggestion, move to the next student and make the same comment. Keep moving down the line until you have spoken to all the students in Group B.
- Decide which piece of advice you like best. Tell the class at the end of the activity.

Group B

- Listen to the problem. Respond with a strong suggestion using the imperative mood. Don't use *should* in your suggestions.

Problems

1. I feel stressed in my everyday life.
2. My wife / husband hates camping, but I love to camp!
3. I love to camp, but I'm afraid to cook outdoors.
4. Campfires are difficult to put out.
5. Sleeping in a tent is so uncomfortable.
6. The silence of the outdoors makes me nervous.
7. I'm tired of working so much. I need a vacation.
8. I don't have a car, but I want to get out into the country.
9. I'm afraid to go into the wild lands.
10. I want to go camping, but I hate to be outside in the rain.

EXAMPLE
A: I feel stressed in my everyday life. What should I do?
B: Don't stay in the city every weekend! Go camping!

WRAP UP

Ⓐ Synthesis

Government messages are often warnings. They try to get the public's attention. They are simple and direct, and they use emotional appeal to get attention.

🎧 *Review the three messages on pages 155–157. Listen to them as you read them. Then work with other students to discuss which emotional appeal is used for each message and fill in the following chart. (There may be more than one emotional appeal used in a message.) The first one has been done for you.*

In Listening 1, humor is used when the mother says, " . . . we'll have to see about that later." Love is expressed when the mother talks to her daughter with affection. For example, she calls her "honey."

Emotional Appeal	Listening 1	Listening 2	Listening 3
Humor	x		
Fear			
Love	x		

B Analysis

The writer of the government safety message in Listening 1 uses a dialogue between a mother and daughter to inform the public about the new law that protects children under age 13 while they are online.

Read the government message in Listening 1 again (pages 155–156). Work in groups. Discuss your answer to the following question:

Is this technique effective? Why or why not?

C Creation

Work with a partner to create a government safety message. Try using the dialogue technique as in Listening 1. Follow the instruction below.

1. Research *one* of the following topics on the Internet or in a library, or choose a topic of your own. Find out about any laws that have been passed. Look for advice that is given to help people live more safely.

   Topics

child safety seats	online shopping	earthquakes
air travel	buying food	hurricanes
highway driving	drinking water	

2. Make your dialogue between one of these pairs of people: (1) a father and son, (2) a husband and wife, or (3) two friends.
3. Be sure to use language studied in this unit (*can / can't,* emphasizing a point, imperative mood) in giving advice.
4. End your safety message with more information. Who can people call? How can people get more information online? Who paid for your message?
5. You may want to role-play your message for the class.

UNIT 5 Love

UNIT 5

Love

Genre: SONGS

Do you have a favorite love song? What is it? What is it about?

Love songs have been popular through the ages. They exist in every language. A love song expresses a singer's joy or sorrow, disappointment or hope. Love songs are usually written with a particular "love" in mind, but we do not always know who that person is.

In this unit, you will listen to three love songs. The singers express different feelings about present and past loves, but they each express a special connection to a special person.

LISTENING 1: "Before I Die" by David Roth

LISTENING 2: "My Lost Valentine" by Cosy Sheridan

LISTENING 3: "The Friendship Waltz" by Lui Collins

59

Work in groups. Discuss your answers to the following questions.

1. What kind of person could you fall in love with? Write five adjectives to describe the qualities you look for.
2. What special wishes might you make before you die?

Ⓐ Vocabulary Preview

Read the following sentences. Guess the meaning of the underlined words. Then match each word with the letter of a definition or synonym from below.

___ 1. Emma loves flowers. She has <u>a wealth of</u> bouquets all around her house.

___ 2. The number of Jonathan's friends was so <u>abundant</u> he couldn't invite everyone to his small apartment.

___ 3. My grandmother was not a great cook, but she always made a great apple <u>pie</u> when we visited her.

___ 4. John's biggest <u>obstacle</u> in life is his shyness. He has a difficult time making friends.

___ 5. Harris has a very stressful job. However, he is able to <u>release</u> his stress when he plays golf on the weekends.

a. dessert; fruit baked in pastry

b. let someone or something go free

c. existing in great numbers

d. a lot of

e. something that makes it difficult for you to succeed

B Listening for the Main Ideas

Listen to the song. Answer the following question. Discuss your answer with a partner.

Which of the following best expresses the theme (main idea) of the song?

    a. The singer is afraid of dying.
    b. The singer wants to reach his goals before he dies.
    c. The singer wants to be rich before he dies.

C Listening for Details

Read the following questions. Listen to the song again. Circle the best answer for each question. Compare your answers with those of another student.

1. How does the singer want to be rich?
    a. with a lot of money
    b. with a lot of friends

2. What kind of lover does he want to find?
    a. one who is soft
    b. one who has a good mind

3. What does he want to do before he dies?
    a. eat a piece of cherry pie
    b. make a cherry pie

4. What does the singer want to choose?
    a. the same life
    b. different experiences

5. How does the singer feel in life right now?
    a. at peace
    b. facing obstacles

6. What does the singer want from his lover?
    a. He wants her to tell him that she loves him.
    b. He wants her to know that he loves her.

D Listening for Inference

Work in pairs. Listen to the excerpt from the song. Answer the questions. Discuss your response with a partner.

1. Why does the singer talk about cherry pie?
2. Why do you think he includes it in his wishes before he dies?

E Discussion

Work in groups. Discuss your answers to the following questions.

1. What four things are most important to the singer? What does he hope to do before he dies? Would you choose similar things? If not, what would you choose?
2. What kind of attitude does the singer express toward life? Toward death? How do these attitudes change with age?

F Looking at Language

Pronunciation: /ay/, /iy/ and / ɪ / sounds

1. *Read the lines from the song as you listen to them. Notice the highlighted words. Each of the words has the vowel sound /ay/, /iy/, or /ɪ/. /ay/ is the vowel sound in* sky, */iy/ is the vowel sound in* meet, *and /ɪ/ is the vowel sound in* fit. *Write /ay/, /iy/ or /ɪ/ above each highlighted word.*

Before **I die I** want to **find**

A lover who **is** soft and **kind**

And one last **piece** of cherry **pie**

That's what **I** want before **I die**

Before **I die I** want to choose

Some **different** roads and avenues

I want to walk **each** one **in peace**

And all my obstacles **release**

The vowel sounds in each of the highlighted words above could easily be confused. In English, the same vowel pronunciation can be spelled differently. For example, in the excerpt above, notice how /ay/ is the sound in both *I* and *pie*, and /iy/ is the sound in both *piece* and *peace*.

In addition, the same letter combinations can produce different sounds in English. For example, the letters *ie* can be pronounced as three different sounds. Compare the difference in pronunciation among the words: *lie*, *thief*, and *sieve*. The *ie* combination produces the /ay/ sound in the word *lie*, the /iy/ sound in the word *thief* and the /ɪ/ sound in the word *sieve*.

It is important to hear the differences among these three vowel sounds. This makes it easier to produce the sounds correctly.

/iy/ is a tense vowel sound. It ends in a /y/ sound. Your lips are spread when you produce this sound.

/ɪ/ is a relaxed (lax) sound. Your lips are not spread when you produce this sound.

/ay/ is a diphthong. The sound changes because the vowel is followed by /y/.

2. Part A: Listen to and repeat the words in each group. (These are all English words, but don't worry if you don't know them.) Part B: Next, listen again and circle the one you hear. Then practice with a partner. Take turns reading one word in each group and checking the one your partner says.

1. **a.** sheen
   b. shine
   c. shin

2. **a.** seen
   b. sign
   c. sin

3. **a.** deal
   b. dial
   c. dill

4. **a.** deem
   b. dime
   c. dim

5. **a.** meal
   b. mile
   c. mill

6. **a.** wheel
   b. while
   c. will

7. **a.** seat
   b. sight
   c. sit

8. **a.** teal
   b. tile
   c. till

LISTENING 2   "MY LOST VALENTINE" BY COSY SHERIDAN

Work in groups. Discuss your answers to the following questions.

1. Valentine's Day, February 14, is the day when people express their love. On this day, many people send roses to the person they love. Why do you think roses symbolize love?

2. People sometimes say, "Love never lasts." What are some common reasons for the end of love between two people?

Ⓐ Vocabulary Preview

Read the following sentences. Guess the meaning of the underlined words. Then choose a definition or synonym for each word.

1. I know that Haley is a happy girl because her face always <u>shines</u>.
   a. looks bright   **b.** looks sad   **c.** looks angry

2. You made a terrible mistake, but I will <u>forgive</u> you this time.
   a. blame   **b.** report   **c.** not be angry with

3. Don't use that knife to cut the bread. Use this one; it's <u>sharper</u>.
   a. heavier   **b.** thicker   **c.** better able to cut

4. In the autumn, my garden is not very pretty because the flowers have all <u>faded</u>.
   a. lost their smell   **b.** lost their color   **c.** lost their taste

5. You can cut some roses for our flower arrangement, but be careful of the <u>thorns</u> on the stems.
   a. leaves   **b.** sharp points   **c.** water

6. I believe love is <u>blind</u>. Even though there are many little things I may not like about my husband, I love him anyway.
   a. perfect   **b.** not realistic   **c.** impossible

Ⓑ Listening for the Main Ideas

Listen to the song. Answer the following question. Discuss your answer with a partner.

Which of the following best expresses the theme (main idea) of the song?

     a. The singer has fallen in love for the first time.
     b. The singer remembers a past love.
     c. The singer asks her love to be her valentine.

Ⓒ Listening for Details

Listen to the song again. Answer the following questions with short answers. Compare your answers with those of another student.

1. If she had sent roses, what would the singer's card have said?

2. Where would she have met her lost valentine?

3. Where would she have held his hand?

4. What is the result of a sweeter bloom?

5. In which month is the "mirror unkind"?

6. What has happened to the flowers at that time of year?

7. Why did she not send her lost valentine roses?

8. What will her lost lover's new valentine someday find?

D **Listening for Inference**

Listen to the excerpt. Notice the highlighted words. Then answer the following questions. Discuss your answers with a partner.

> i would have sent you roses
> but it would not be kind
> to whoever it is,
> is your **this year's valentine**
> who must someday find the **thorn**
> that you **prefer your love blind**
> roses, my lost valentine
> roses

1. What does the singer mean by "this year's valentine"? Who might this person be?
2. Why will this year's valentine have to find a "thorn"? What does a thorn represent if we are talking about a person?
3. Why does her lost love "prefer [his] love blind"? What does it mean to be blind in love? What does this say about the person the singer is singing to?

E **Discussion**

Work in groups. Discuss your answers to the following questions.

1. The singer and her love did not stay together. What things does she regret? What would she have liked to do?
2. Express the song in your own words. What is the message of the songwriter? Is her experience a common experience?

F **Looking at Language**

Grammar: Double Comparatives

1. *Read the line from the song. What is the singer saying about the relationship between the bloom and the vine?*

> but the sweeter the bloom, the sharper the vine

In the previous line from the song, the singer uses the comparative to show a cause-and-effect relationship. She sings that if the bloom (rose) is sweet, its vine is sharp. One causes the other. If there is more of one thing, there is more of the other thing.

To form a comparative:

Add -er to short adjectives (one syllable) (*sweeter, colder, blinder*).

Add *more* in front of two-syllable adjectives (*more faded*).

For two-syllable adjectives that end in -y, change the -y to -i and add -er (*happier*).

The	Comparative Form	the	Comparative Form
The	sweeter the bloom,	the	sharper the vine.
The	colder the winter,	the	more faded the flowers.
The	blinder the love,	the	happier the lover.

2. *The following sentences describe conditions for happiness in love. Complete the sentences using the structures in the chart.*

1. Not everyone agrees that _____ (wealthy) the couple, the _____ (happy) the marriage.

2. Many people are looking for that perfect mate. However, **most people realize** that _____ (kind) the person, _____ (successful) the relationship.

3. When baking pies, my mother always looked for ripe fruit. _____ (sweet) the cherries, _____ (tasty) the pie!

4. People say separation can keep love strong. So, does that **mean that** _____ (distant) your partner, _____ (good) the relationship?

5. "Beauty is only skin deep" doesn't mean _____ (pretty) the girl, _____ (beautiful) the person. It means that **beauty is** deeper than what we see on the outside.

6. There must be more than romance to make love last a long time. Most people agree that _____ (strong) the friendship, _____ (deep) the love.

7. People say love comes easy when you are young and innocent. _____ (blind) the love, _____ (easy) the romance.

www.susanwilsonphoto.com

Work in groups. Discuss your answers to the following questions.

1. Why do good friends sometimes separate? What happens?
2. Have you ever lost a good friend? Why are you no longer together? How do you feel about that person now?

A Vocabulary Preview

Read the following diary entry. Guess the meaning of the underlined words. Then match the number of each word with a definition or synonym from below.

> Dear Diary,
>
> Last night, I went to the school dance with James and Sarah. We were out all night, and I didn't get home until (1) dawn! While I was dancing with James, I saw someone I recognized! Her (2) presence at this dance was totally unexpected. It was my old friend Natasha, walking into the room. I knew (3) on sight that it was my friend, and I had to (4) grin! I was so happy to see her again after so long! Even though our (5) paths had separated years ago, I recognized her immediately. She had come back to visit her old friends at our school. Something had (6) drawn her back to us.
>
> It's so hard to accept the (7) longing we feel for friends we have lost. I had waited (8) patiently to see Natasha again, but I was never sure whether or not she would be back in my life. I hope that we will be friends again. It was always an (9) honor to have her as a friend.

____ **a.** ways in which people go   ____ **f.** immediately

____ **b.** something that makes you feel proud   ____ **g.** smile

____ **c.** strong feeling of wanting   ____ **h.** calmly, with acceptance

____ **d.** when the sun rises   ____ **i.** the state of being present in a particular place

____ **e.** pulled

B Listening for the Main Ideas

Listen to the song. Answer the following question. Discuss your answer with a partner.

Which of the following best expresses the theme (main idea) of the song?

    a. The singer and her friend no longer see each other.
    b. The singer's friend died.
    c. The singer and her friend are getting back together after a separation.

C Listening for Details

Read the following questions. Listen to the song again. Circle the best answer for each question. Compare your answers with those of another student.

  1. How would the singer welcome her friend?
    a. with a smile
    b. with a laugh

  2. What can the singer see?
    a. her friend's sweet smile
    b. her friend's eyes

  3. How does the singer feel about their paths drawn apart?
    a. She understands it.
    b. She is angry that they are no longer together.

  4. Why are these friends no longer together?
    a. They chose to be distant.
    b. One friend left the other.

  5. What do these friends share?
    a. the same space
    b. honor

D Listening for Inference

The singer begins and ends on the same refrain. A refrain is a repetition of a group of words in a song.

Read the first and last refrain of the song as you listen to it. Notice that the singer changes the verb form in the last refrain. How does the verb form change the meaning at the end of the song? What is she saying about her friend? Discuss your answer with a partner.

First refrain: I **would welcome** your presence back into my life
    With an ear to ear grin I **would greet** you on sight
    I **would dance** until dawn, I **would laugh** at the rain
    I **would welcome** your friendship again.

Last refrain:	And then I'**ll welcome** your presence back into my life
	And with an ear to ear grin I **shall greet** you on sight
	I **will dance** until dawn, I **will laugh** at the rain
	I **will welcome** your friendship again
	I **will welcome** your friendship again.

Ⓔ Discussion

Work in groups. Discuss your answers to the following questions.

1. Do you think the singer will get back with her friend? Or is her song just a wish, a beautiful idea? Why do you think so?

2. Think of a friend you do not see anymore. What attitude do you usually have toward a friend who is no longer in your life? Do you move on and forget? Do you just wait and hope that your friend will come back into your life? Do you call or write your friend and try and get that person to be your friend again?

Ⓕ Looking at Language

Function: Acknowledging Another Person's Point of View

1. *Read the following lines from the song. Which is the singer's main idea, the first line or the second line? What do you think the first line means?*

Though I well understand our paths drawn apart,
I still feel the longing deep in my heart.

When speakers want to recognize another person's point of view before giving their own, they often acknowledge the other person's view first. It softens the main point they want to make. The listener is more ready to hear what they have to say.

On page 70 are some other phrases that acknowledge another's point of view. We use them before expressing an opposite point of view. Notice that the phrases in Group A use a subordinating conjunction to introduce another's point of view; the phrases in Group B use a coordinating conjunction to connect the speaker's point of view.

Group A	Group B
Though . . . ,	*I know it's true that . . . , but . . .*
Although . . . ,	*I understand that . . . , but . . .*
Even though . . . ,	*I can see that . . . , but . . .*
While . . . ,	
Whereas . . . ,	
In spite of the fact that . . . ,	

 EXAMPLE A

<u>Even though</u> we must be apart, I will always love you!

EXAMPLE B

I understand that we must be apart, <u>but</u> I will always love you!

2. *Read the following mini-dialogues. Write a response using a phrase from the lists above. Then read the dialogues with a partner.*

EXAMPLE

A: I never see you anymore.

B: Even though you never see me anymore, we will always be friends!

1. A: I think we need to spend some time apart.

   B: _____ , I know we will always honor and respect each other.

2. A: I want to spend my life with you!

   B: _____ , but we are still young and need to accomplish our individual goals.

3. A: I haven't seen my friend in years.

   B: _____ , you will always be friends.

4. A: Your friend moved far away!

   B: _____ , I am still patiently waiting her return.

5. A: My friend and I share a promise to always be there.

   B: _____ , but I wonder if you will really see your friend again.

WRAP UP

A Synthesis

1. *Songwriters often refer to the five senses (sight, smell, taste, sound, and touch), especially in love songs. Read the songs on pages 157–158 again. Mark the senses that are mentioned in each song in the following chart. Write an explanation for your answers. For example, point out the vocabulary in the song that expresses the sense. The first one has been done for you.*

	Sight	Smell	Taste	Sound	Touch
Song 1			X	X	X

Explanation: *The singer mentions "cherry pie," which is a memory of taste. He also wants to be sure he has "told" his love that he loves her, which is a sound; he must use his words. He also talks about a lover who is "soft," which refers to touch.*

Song 2

Explanation:

Song 3

Explanation:

2. *Love songs are often written when the writer has difficulty expressing his or her love to someone. In which song do you think the singer has the most trouble expressing his or her love to the other person? Why? Explain your choice by giving examples from the songs.*

B Analysis

Love songs, like many songs, usually have leitmotifs. A leitmotif is a part of a song that is repeated at different times in the song. Each of the three songs has a leitmotif, but the leitmotifs appear in different places in the songs.

Work with another student. Read the songs on pages 157–158. Answer the following questions. Write some notes in the following chart. The first one has been done for you.

	Song 1 "Before I Die"	Song 2 "My Lost Valentine"	Song 3 "The Friendship Waltz"
1. How many leitmotifs are there?	2		
2. Where are the leitmotifs in the song?	First two lines of first and last stanzas; last two lines of second and last stanza		
3. What meaning does the leitmotif give to the song?	Important things singer wants before death		

C Creation

Write the lyrics for a love song. Think of someone special (a love, a family member, a friend). Write lyrics to express your feelings to that person.

Include a leitmotif in your song. Consider the different ways to do this from your work in Section B above. Try to use language from the Looking at Language sections in your songwriting. You may want to record your song and play it for the class.

6 Volunteering

Genre: PUBLIC SERVICE ANNOUNCEMENTS

These three young people are the recipients of the Yoshiyama Award for Exemplary Service to the Community.

Do people where you live give their time to help other people? What kinds of things do they do?

Public service announcements (PSAs) are short radio or television reports. They send a social message to the public. They are similar to commercials, but they are educational. They give important information. They often ask people to give some of their time to help other people in need.

In this unit, you will hear three PSAs produced by young adults. Each PSA focuses on a different subject, but all three ask us to think about getting involved to help other people.

LISTENING 1: "Discover the Joy in Serving Others" by Amber Coffman

LISTENING 2: "Find One Hour a Week" by Regina Grant

LISTENING 3: "A Need to Fill" by Wrex Phipps

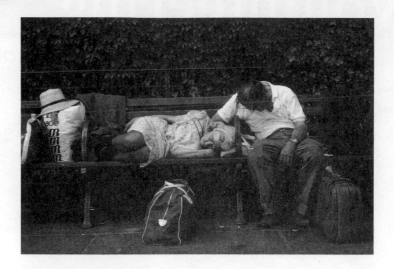

Work in groups. Discuss your answers to the following questions.

1. Look at the picture. What kind of life do these people have? Why are they living this way?
2. What can be done to help them? Give some suggestions.

Ⓐ Vocabulary Preview

Read the following sentences. Guess the meaning of the underlined words. Then match each word with the letter of a definition or synonym from page 75.

____ 1. No one can pay the high rents in this city! That's why there are more and more <u>homeless</u> people living on the street.

____ 2. That public radio station is a <u>nonprofit</u> business, so it has to ask listeners for money.

____ 3. Every day the mail is <u>delivered</u> to his house at 3 P.M.

____ 4. Matt never helped around the house, so his father was <u>amazed</u> when Matt said he would wash the dishes.

____ 5. I know you think you can't climb to the top of this mountain, but if you <u>put your mind to it</u>, you can do it!

____ 6. It is important for students to learn the value of helping others, so more and more teachers are asking their students to <u>volunteer</u> in their school or community.

____ 7. If you give your time and love to an older person, you can really <u>make a difference</u> in that person's life.

a. offer to do something without expecting to be paid
b. not having a place to live
c. very surprised
d. uses the money it earns to help people
e. taken to a certain place
f. are determined to do something
g. improve a situation

Ⓑ Listening for the Main Ideas

Listen to the PSA. Answer the following question and discuss with a partner.

What does Amber's organization do?

Ⓒ Listening for Details

Read the following statements. Listen to the PSA again. Mark the statements T (true) or F (false). Compare your answers with those of another student.

_____ **1.** Amber was eight years old when she realized what she had to do.

_____ **2.** She started a profit group to feed the homeless.

_____ **3.** Amber's organization is called Happy Helpers for the Homeless.

_____ **4.** Homeless people come to her home for food and clothing.

_____ **5.** Amber helps other young people discover the joy in serving others.

_____ **6.** Amber thinks people know there's something they need to do in their communities.

_____ **7.** People often think, "I'm sure I can do something to help."

_____ **8.** Amber thinks we can make a difference if we put our minds to it.

Ⓓ Listening for Inference

Listen to the excerpt from Amber's PSA. What does Amber mean by this? Check (✓) the possible interpretations. Discuss your answers with a partner.

_____ **1.** We feel lazy.

_____ **2.** We feel scared.

_____ **3.** We feel uninterested.

_____ **4.** We feel helpless.

_____ **5.** We feel separated from the problem.

_____ **6.** We feel lonely.

E Discussion

Work in groups. Discuss your answers to the following questions.

1. Would you volunteer to help the homeless, as Amber did? If not, would you volunteer to help some other group of people?

2. Why do people volunteer? Why do people *not* volunteer?

F Looking at Language

Grammar: Modals of Obligation

1. *Read the excerpt from the PSA. What is the meaning of the highlighted words?*

> I was eight years old when I realized what it was that I **had to do**.
> I was walking down the street, and I saw so many homeless
> men and women. I knew I **had to find a** way to help.

Had to is the past form of the modal *have to,* a modal of obligation. *Have to* has the same meaning as *must*.

The modals of obligation in the following chart have different degrees of obligation.

	Modal	Notes on Usage/Meaning	Examples
Strong	*must*	obligation/necessity	You **must** send your application by January 10.
		past form of must = had to	
		not normally used in questions	
		negative form = prohibition (different meaning)	You **must** not drive over 55 miles per hour. (It's against the law.)
	have to	obligation / necessity	I have to finish my homework tonight.
		used more frequently in everyday speech	
	had better	obligation / warning	You **had better** study, or you will fail the exam.
		often gives a warning of bad consequences	
		not normally used in questions	
	have got to	obligation	
		generally used in informal speech and writing past form = had to	Look what time it is! We **have got to** start making dinner!
	should / ought to	obligation / advice	
Weak		modal of obligation when talking about oneself (only used in present tense for this meaning)	I **should** pay my bills today.

2. Work in pairs. Student A reads the question or comment. Student B responds with the most appropriate modal of obligation. Change roles after item 4.

1. **A:** Why are you working so late?
   B: I (have to / should) finish this report before tomorrow's meeting. Otherwise, my boss will be very angry.

2. **A:** Jack called and invited me to the movies, mom.
   B: You (ought to / had better) finish your homework first, or you will not be going out tonight!

3. **A:** Did you volunteer for school this semester?
   B: I (must not / don't have to) volunteer this semester. It's not required.

4. **A:** Did you see all the homeless people living on my street?
   B: Maybe you (had better / should) get more involved with your community. I'm sure you could do something to help.

Now change roles.

5. **A:** You don't really enjoy your work anymore, do you?
   B: I know. I guess I (must / should) consider getting another job.

6. **A:** Why don't you get more involved with your community?
   B: You're right. Perhaps I (ought to / have to) find some time each week to volunteer.

7. **A:** What's written on that notice?
   B: It says that I (must not / ought not to) park here or my car will be towed next time.

8. **A:** Why are you spending so much time volunteering at the homeless shelter?
   B: I feel that I (have to / had better) do something to contribute to society. It makes me feel good.

Photo courtesy of Dartmouth College

Work in groups. Discuss your answers to the following questions.

1. Look at the picture. What kind of life do you think young Native Americans have in the United States?
2. Do any minority groups (people of different backgrounds) live in your country? Do they have any problems? What kind of help do they need?

Ⓐ Vocabulary Preview

Read the definitions of the following words and phrases. Then complete the sentences with the best word or phrase.

support system:	people who support a person through difficult times
to be somebody:	to be important or to do something that others notice
graduate:	obtain a degree from a college, university, or high school
tribe:	a social group that lives in one area ruled by a chief
mentors:	people who advise and help less experienced people
heritage:	traditional beliefs, values, customs, and so on of a family, country, or society
commit:	use all of the time and energy that you can in order to achieve something

1. Josh failed two of his final exams, so he was worried that he might not _____ in June.

2. There are only a few members of that Native American _____ who still live in this community.

3. You only have to _____ a few hours each week to be a volunteer at the hospital.

4. Even though Joyce had grown up poor, she had a strong _____. Her family gave her much love and helped her do well in school.

5. My cousin always wanted _____. He has dreamed of being a famous doctor or lawyer ever since he was very young.

6. Many immigrants lose some of their _____ when they go to live in another country.

7. Joe had several _____ when he was growing up, which made it easier to grow up without a father at home.

Ⓑ Listening for the Main Ideas

Listen to the PSA. Answer the following question. Discuss your answer with a partner.

What does Regina's program do?

Ⓒ Listening for Details

Read the following statements. Listen to the PSA again. Mark the statements T (true) or F (false). Compare your answers with those of another student.

____ **1.** Regina felt lucky growing up.

____ **2.** She felt she could be somebody.

____ **3.** She didn't understand why other kids couldn't be somebody.

____ **4.** Regina is a member of the Umonhon tribe.

____ **5.** She thinks Native Americans cannot be successful in college.

____ **6.** She thinks it's important that Native American kids know about their heritage.

____ **7.** Young people commit one hour a week of their time to volunteer in her program.

____ **8.** Many people in every community need help.

Ⓓ Listening for Inference

Regina expresses some ideas without saying them explicitly. Listen to her PSA again. Mark the following statements T(true) or F(false). Discuss your answers with a partner.

____ **1.** Regina thinks she is luckier than most Native Americans.

____ **2.** Many Native Americans don't think they can be successful in college.

____ **3.** Most Native Americans know their heritage well.

____ **4.** The young people in her program don't volunteer enough time.

____ **5.** One hour a week of volunteer work in your community can make a difference.

E Discussion

Work in groups. Discuss your answers to the following questions.

1. Why do you think going to college is a problem for Native American kids? Why does Regina feel she needs to help them?
2. Why do you think volunteers teach Native American kids about where they come from? Why do you think they need to do this?

F Looking at Language

Function: Persuading

1. *Read the excerpt from the PSA. What is the purpose of the highlighted expression?*

> The young people who volunteer to be mentors in our program commit just one hour a week of their time. **Couldn't you find** one hour a week to volunteer in something you believe in?

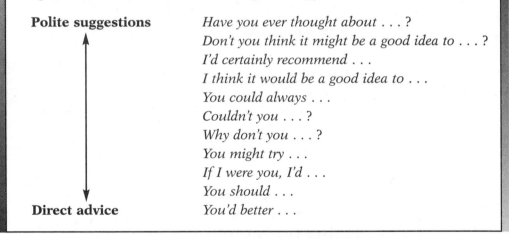

The purpose of a PSA is to get people to do something. When we want to make suggestions to persuade people to do things for their community or for their own good, there are several expressions we can use. The following expressions are listed in order from polite suggestions to direct advice:

Polite suggestions

Have you ever thought about . . . ?
Don't you think it might be a good idea to . . . ?
I'd certainly recommend . . .
I think it would be a good idea to . . .
You could always . . .
Couldn't you . . . ?
Why don't you . . . ?
You might try . . .
If I were you, I'd . . .
You should . . .
You'd better . . .

Direct advice

2. *Work in groups of four. Each student reads a different situation about a community problem and asks the other students in the group for advice. The other students give polite suggestions or direct advice using expressions from the list above.*

Student A's Situation

There are more and more homeless people living in my city. So many people have lost their jobs, and they can't afford to pay rent. They ask for money or food on the street everyday. I can see that they are hungry. It's very depressing. What can be done about the situation?

Student B's Situation

The transportation system is not good in my town. There are only a few buses that run on the main streets. This is a big problem for older people who can no longer drive. They stay in their homes, and they have to depend on people to drive them. How can we improve this situation?

Student C's Situation

I live in an immigrant community. Many of my neighbors have teenage children who are dropping out of school. They don't see how a college education can help them. They want to find a job and earn money, but the jobs they find never pay very much. How can we help them understand the importance of a college education?

Student D's Situation

There is a big problem with street gangs in my community. Teenagers hang out on the streets, and they often join gangs that commit crimes. Lots of young people join these gangs because there isn't much to do in my town. Kids are bored. They don't have a good family life, so the street gang becomes their family. I'm worried that the problem is getting worse. What are some solutions?

LISTENING 3 "A NEED TO FILL" BY WREX PHIPPS

Work in groups. Discuss your answers to the following questions.

1. What kinds of jobs are dangerous? What kinds of accidents can happen in these jobs?
2. Do young people work on farms in your country? Why or why not?

A Vocabulary Preview

Read the following sentences. Guess the meaning of the underlined words. Then choose a definition or synonym for each word.

1. For years we have been looking for a cure for cancer, a <u>deadly</u> disease.
   - **a.** likely to cause death
   - **b.** very old

2. Farming today would be difficult without a <u>tractor</u> to work in the fields.
   - **a.** large horse
   - **b.** strong vehicle

3. My grandparents moved to the United States in hopes of finding the <u>American Dream</u>, but life was difficult for them and they couldn't find work for many months.
   - **a.** successful life
   - **b.** exciting life

4. When Dan saw the children building a tree house, he <u>was reminded of</u> his own childhood.
   - **a.** became interested in
   - **b.** remembered

5. Many people <u>avoid</u> doing volunteer work because they think one person can't make a difference.
   - **a.** try
   - **b.** stay away from

6. Your children are too young to go away to overnight camp this summer, but there are many good <u>day camps</u> in town.
   - **a.** places where children go for special activities for the day
   - **b.** places where parents meet each other

7. I love to travel to different countries, but I especially love the feeling of going back to visit my <u>hometown</u>.
   - **a.** place where you were born or lived when you were a child
   - **b.** parents' place of origin

B Listening for the Main Ideas

Listen to the PSA. Answer the following question. Discuss your answer with a partner.

Which group of people is Wrex helping?

C Listening for Details

Listen to the PSA again. Circle the best answer to complete each sentence. Discuss your answers with a partner.

1. When Wrex was growing up on a farm, he thought his life was ___.
   - **a.** deadly
   - **b.** great

2. He had his own ___.
   - **a.** horse
   - **b.** tractor

3. For him, the American Dream was ___.
   - **a.** city life
   - **b.** farm life

4. His American Dream changed when ___ .
    a. he was almost killed   **b.** his cousin was almost killed

5. He decided that he could ___ .
    a. help his cousin   **b.** help other people

6. Wrex volunteered ___ .
    a. at a farm   **b.** at a day camp for children

7. He taught people ___ .
    a. how to be safe   **b.** how to farm

8. Wrex thinks we need to ___ .
    a. help our community   **b.** change our community

Ⓓ Listening for Inference

Listen to the excerpt from the PSA. Answer the questions. Discuss your answers with a partner.

1. Why does Wrex say his life was "the American Dream"? What does he mean?
2. What values do you think he is thinking of?

Ⓔ Discussion

Work in groups. Discuss your answers to the following questions.

1. Is working on a farm "the American Dream," in your opinion? Why or why not?
2. Wrex says, "Find out how you can help in your hometown." What kinds of needs does your community have? Can you help?

Ⓕ Looking at Language

Pronunciation: Listing Intonation

1. *Read the excerpt from the PSA as you listen to it. Focus on the list of things mentioned for farm safety. Do the highlighted words have a rising (⌣) or falling (⌢) intonation?*

> So I volunteered at farm safety day camps for children of all ages, teaching kids about being safe around **tractors, tools,** and **animals.**

When speakers list items, they tend to use a rising intonation for each item until they finish. When we hear the word *animals,* we know that the speaker is finished with his list of examples because of his rise / fall intonation pattern at the end. The conjunction *and* or *or* usually introduces the final item of the list.

If a speaker wants to show that there could be more items in the list (but maybe can't think of them right now), all items end on a rising intonation, indicating that list is unfinished. If Wrex had wanted to include more items on his list, each word would end on a rising intonation:

So I volunteered at farm safety day camps for children of all ages,

teaching kids about being safe around tractors, tools, animals . . . "

2. *Imagine that Wrex Phipps is being interviewed about his experience. Listen to the following mini-dialogues between an interviewer and Wrex Phipps. Draw the intonation patterns for each underlined item in Wrex Phipps's response. If the items are an unfinished list and end on a rising intonation, punctuate the sentence with three dots (. . .). If the items are a finished list and end on a rise / fall intonation, punctuate the sentence with a period (.).*

Work in pairs. Practice reading the dialogues with the correct intonation patterns. Change roles.

1. Interviewer: Why was your life on the farm so great?

Wrex Phipps: I had a horse, drove a tractor, worked with my dad

2. Interviewer: Why did you feel like you were living the American Dream?

Wrex Phipps: I lived on a farm, spent time with my family, and worked very hard

3. Interviewer: When did your life change?

Wrex Phipps: My life changed when my cousin was almost killed, when I couldn't do anything to help him, and when I realized how dangerous farm work could be

4. Interviewer: Who do you work with when you volunteer?

Wrex Phipps: Oh, kids of all ages: preschool children, grade school kids, high school kids

5. Interviewer: What kinds of safety issues do you teach the kids?

Wrex Phipps: They need to learn about being safe around tractors, using tools correctly, taking care of animals

6. Interviewer: What do you think we can do?

Wrex Phipps: Just like me, you can fill a need in your community, find out how you can help in your hometown, get out and volunteer

WRAP UP

Ⓐ Synthesis

Work in groups. Review the information in the three PSAs. Fill in the on page 85 chart with the following information.

- Which group of people is being served? Who are the *people in need?*
- What kinds of *problems* does this group have? (What is mentioned in the PSA?)
- What kinds of *solutions* are offered? (What is mentioned in the PSA?)
- What other ideas can you think of to help this group of people?

	People in Need	Problems	Solutions	Your Ideas
PSA 1: Amber Coffman				
PSA 2: Regina Grant				
PSA 3: Wrex Phipps				

B Analysis

The PSAs in this unit use the same structure: (1) The speaker tells an anecdote, or personal story, to explain how he or she became a volunteer; (2) the speaker explains his or her organization or program; (3) the speaker makes an appeal to us (the listeners) to volunteer.

Work in groups. Take notes on the three parts of each PSA in the following chart. Discuss the strengths of each PSA.

PSA	Anecdote (Personal Story)	Description of Organization	Appeal to Listeners
PSA 1			
PSA 2			
PSA 3			

C Creation

Work in pairs. Consider problems in your own community. (These could be problems of individuals, specific groups, or the whole society.) Choose one for a PSA and follow the instructions below.

1. Write a PSA that focuses on a problem in your community. Include an anecdote, or personal experience, in your PSA (something you saw, someone you know, and so on). Imagine that you have set up an organization or volunteer group. Describe your organization and what you do. Make an appeal to get others to volunteer. (Use language from the Section Fs in this unit.)
2. Read your PSA to the class or record your PSA at home and play it for the class.

7 Life Lessons

This is a picture from the famous fable, "The Tortoise and the Hare."

What fables, or short stories, are famous in your culture? What do they try to teach people?

Storytelling is a very old art form. Even as our world becomes more modernized, storytelling is still a popular form of entertainment. Today both children and adults are enjoying stories that teach us life lessons. These stories offer solutions to common problems.

In this unit, you will hear three fables. Fables are traditional short stories, often about animals, that teach a moral lesson. These stories teach us practical lessons about what to do or how to behave. All three stories were told by storytellers on *The Kojo Nnamdi Show* on WAMC radio.

LISTENING 1: "The Dove and the Ant" by Diane Macklin

LISTENING 2: "The Prince Who Thought He Was a Rooster" by Renee Brachfeld and Mark Novak

LISTENING 3: "The Lady in the Pot" by Marc Spiegel

Diane Macklin telling a story

Work in groups. Discuss your answers to the following question.

Have you ever helped someone you didn't think you could ever help? Tell the story.

Ⓐ Vocabulary Preview

Work in small groups. Match the words below to the pictures. Write the letter on the line. Use a dictionary only if necessary.

a.

b.

c.

d.

e.

f.

g.

h.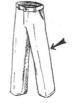

i.

____ **1.** tiny   ____ **4.** pants leg   ____ **7.** hunter

____ **2.** drown   ____ **5.** shore   ____ **8.** ant

____ **3.** howl   ____ **6.** dove   ____ **9.** crawl

GENRE: Storytelling ■ 87

B Listening for the Main Ideas

Listen to the story. Answer the following question. Discuss your answer with a partner.

Which of the following best expresses the main idea?

    a. The ant and dove helped each other.
    b. The ant helped the dove, but the dove couldn't help the ant.
    c. The dove helped the ant, but the ant couldn't help the dove.

C Listening for Details

Read the following statements. Listen to the story again. Number the events in the order in which they happened. Write a number from 1 to 9 next to each event. The first one has been done for you.

____   The hunter howled.

____   The ant told the dove she would help her one day.

____   A hunter came along.

____   The dove thanked the ant for changing her life.

1   The dove heard a little, tiny voice calling out.

____   The dove didn't notice that the hunter was going to shoot her.

____   The ant climbed up the hunter's pants leg and bit him.

____   The dove flew down and rescued the ant.

____   The dove flew away and was saved from the hunter.

D Listening for Inference

Fables usually have a moral, a practical lesson that teaches us how to live. Listen to the fable again. Complete the following sentence. Discuss your answer with a partner.

The moral of the story is _____

_____

E Discussion

Work in groups. Discuss your answers to the following questions.

1. Did you like the story? Why or why not?
2. In this story, something small and weak helps something big and strong. Do you know other stories like this? If so, share your stories.

F Looking at Language

Pronunciation: Diphthongs

1. *Read the excerpt from the fable as you listen to it. Notice the vowel sound of the highlighted word. Describe the vowel sound. Is it a pure vowel sound, or does the vowel sound change from one sound to another?*

> And when that ant saw that hunter, she crawled over to him, climbed up his pants leg, and bit him. **"Ow!"** That hunter howled in the air.

> The sound above is not a pure vowel sound. It is a diphthong. In English there are three diphthongs. Diphthongs are vowels followed by /w/ or /y/. The vowel starts as one vowel sound and ends as another sound.
>
> Listen to the pronunciation of the three English diphthongs:
>
> **/aw/** One day a dove was sitting on the <u>bough</u> of a tree, when she heard a <u>loud</u> noise <u>down</u> in the river.
>
> **/ay/** The dove heard the ant's <u>cry</u>, and flew down from her <u>high</u> branch to save the ant from <u>dying</u>.
>
> **/oy/** When the ant heard the <u>noise</u> of the hunter coming along, she made the <u>choice</u> to climb up his pants leg to <u>annoy</u> him.

2. *Work in pairs. Listen to the following sentences from the story. Which diphthong is in each highlighted word? Place each word in the diphthong chart that follows. Then practice reading the sentences to each other. Focus on the pronunciation of the diphthongs.*

   1. There was a dove who was perched on a branch, enjoying the wonderful summer day, when she heard a little, **tiny voice** calling out, "Help me. Help me."
   2. She flew **down** and rescued that ant and put her on the shore. "Ant, friend, the river is no place for you. You could have **drowned**."
   3. And there was a hunter that came along, and the dove was just admiring the **sky** and **enjoying** the day so much that she did not notice that hunter.
   4. And when that ant saw that hunter, she crawled over to him, **climbed** up his pants leg, and bit him. **"Ow!"** That hunter **howled** in the air.
   5. Later on that day, the dove came over and **found** that ant and she said, "Oh, thank you, ant. Thank you."

/aw/	/ay/	/oy/

by Renee Brachfeld and Mark Novak

Mark Novak and Renee Brachfeld, storytellers

Work in groups. Discuss your answers to the following questions.

Have you ever asked for help or advice from someone who wasn't a friend or family member? Why or why not?

Ⓐ Vocabulary Preview

Read the following sentences. Guess the meaning of the underlined words. Then match each word with the letter of a definition or synonym from page 91.

_____ **1.** I loved to visit my grandparents' farm when I was a child. Every morning I would wake up to the <u>rooster</u> crowing "cock-a-doodle-do!"

_____ **2.** Each spring my dog <u>sheds</u> his winter coat, and there is dog hair everywhere!

_____ **3.** The children <u>crouched</u> down behind the sofa to hide from their friends.

_____ **4.** Each morning the farmer feeds his chickens <u>kernels of corn</u>.

_____ **5.** The police are offering a huge <u>reward</u> for information about the robbery.

_____ **6.** The doctors did everything they could do to help the patient, but they couldn't <u>cure</u> her, and she died.

_____ **7.** The supervisor was <u>suspicious</u> of her employee when she found him sitting at her desk and using her computer one morning.

_____ **8.** Tyler was the most popular kid in the class, so the other children tried to <u>imitate</u> him.

_____ **9.** When Natalie's parents heard that she had got an A on her exam, they were <u>overjoyed</u>.

a. the seeds you can eat on an ear of corn
b. male chicken
c. something, especially an amount of money, that is given to someone for doing something good, such as providing information
d. extremely happy because something good has happened
e. to make an illness or disease go away
f. loses
g. not willing to trust someone or something
h. lowered their bodies close to the ground by bending their knees and back
i. do something in exactly the same way as someone or something else

B Listening for the Main Ideas

 Listen to the story. Answer the following questions. Discuss your answers with a partner.

1. What was wrong with the prince?
   a. He was a rooster and wanted to be a human.
   b. He was a rooster and wanted to stay a rooster.
   c. He was a human and wanted to be a rooster.

2. What happened at the end of the story?
   a. The wise man could not cure the prince.
   b. The wise man cured the prince.
   c. The wise man decided to be a rooster.

C Listening for Details

Read the following questions. Listen to the story again. Answer the questions with short answers. Compare your answers with those of another student.

1. What was the only thing the prince ate?

2. What did the king offer the person who could cure his son?

3. How much time did the wise man ask to spend with the prince?

4. What three things did the wise man do when he went into the room with the prince the first time?

5. How did the prince react to the wise man's actions?

6. What relationship did the wise man and the prince have after this?

7. How did the prince first react when the wise man put his fancy robes back on?

8. What three things did the prince finally do?

9. How did the king react to his son?

10. What did the wise man get in the end?

D Listening for Inference

Fables usually have a moral, a practical lesson that teaches us how to live. Listen to the fable again. Answer the following question. Discuss your answer with a partner.

Which statement best describes the moral of this story?

   a. Never trust a person who seems to be wiser than you.
   b. To help someone, you must first find a way to get that person's trust.
   c. A person's outside appearance may not show his inside beauty.

E Discussion

Work in groups. Discuss your answers to the following questions.

1. Why are many fables or stories about kings and queens, princes and princesses? Why do people love these stories?
2. "The Prince Who Thought He Was a Rooster" could be a modern-day story. What does this story tell us about people's relationships today? Who could the prince be? Who could the wise man be?

F Looking at Language

Function: Time Order

1. *Read the excerpt from the story as you listen to it. Focus on the highlighted phrases. What function do they serve in telling the story?*

> **After another day or so had passed**, the wise man crawled out from under the table. He began to walk around the room, standing upright, straight and tall, like a man. The prince was beside himself. "Roosters just don't get up and walk around like that!" "I'm a rooster, and I can walk like this if I choose to," insisted the wise man. The prince thought about this, too, **and after a short time** decided to imitate his friend. And he, too, walked. And so it was. **By the end of the week**, the prince no longer acted like a rooster. He wore clothes and ate food and walked like a man.

> When telling a story, speakers use phrases of *time order* to connect events. These phrases help the listener understand what happened and when. They provide a clear past, present, and future reference. Here are some useful phrases speakers can use when telling stories:

To indicate same time as an event

all of a sudden
at that moment
one day, morning, evening
at this point
that morning

To indicate earlier time than an event

sometime before
earlier that day
the day before

To indicate time that follows an event

then
afterward
after a little while
later
much later
finally

2. *Read the following summary of "The Prince Who Thought He Was a Rooster." Use phrases from the preceding lists to connect the sequence of events where they are needed. Then work in pairs. Read your summary with time order phrases to your partner.*

There was a prince who thought he was a rooster. He spent his days crouched beneath a table, eating corn. (**1**) _____ his father, the king, called for a doctor. (**2**) _____ a wise man passed through the kingdom. He asked the king to give him a week with his son. The wise man went into the prince's room. He shed his robes. He crouched beneath the table. He ate kernels of corn. (**3**) _____ the suspicious prince asked him, "Who are you?" The wise man said, "I am a rooster." (**4**) _____ they both cried, "Cock-a-doodle doo!" The two became good friends. (**5**)

_____ the wise man crawled out from under the table. He put his robes back on. The prince was very upset. He said, "Roosters don't wear clothes like that!" The wise man said he could dress the way he wanted. (**6**)

_____ the prince imitated his friend. (**7**) _____

the wise man crawled out from under the table. He ate delicious food. The prince was disgusted. He said, "Roosters don't eat that kind of food!" The wise man said he could eat any kind of food he liked. (8) _____ the prince imitated his friend.(9) _____ the wise man crawled out from under the table. He began to walk around the room. The prince said, "Roosters don't get up and walk around like that!" The wise man insisted that he could if he wanted to. (10) _____ the prince imitated his friend. (11) _____ the prince no longer acted like a rooster. The king was overjoyed. The wise man collected his large reward. He went happily on his way.

LISTENING 3   "THE LADY IN THE POT" BY MARC SPIEGEL

Marc Spiegel, telling a story

Work in groups. Discuss your answers to the following questions.

Have you ever misjudged a person? In other words, have you ever not liked a person at first . . . but later liked that person very much? Why? What happened?

A Vocabulary Preview

Read the definitions of the following words. Then complete the sentences with the best word.

adorned:	formally decorated
basement:	room in a building that is below the level of the ground
smashed:	made to break into many small pieces violently
straddling:	sitting or standing with your legs on either side of something
rim:	outside edge of something circular, such as a glass or a wheel
pin:	a piece of jewelry fastened to your clothes
banjo:	a musical instrument with four or more strings, a circular body, and a long neck
floated:	moved up into the air without falling

1. The lamp fell from the table and _____ into tiny pieces.

2. The child let go of his balloons, so they _____ up into the sky.

3. I don't want an apartment in the _____ of a building. I need to have plenty of sunlight where I live.

4. Waiter! Please get me another glass. The _____ on this one is dirty.

5. The country band had three musicians who played the guitar, the _____ , and the drums.

6. The prince was _____ with beautiful robes and a crown on his head.

7. We saw the bicyclists _____ their mountain bikes, waiting for the race to begin.

8. Justin's teacher loves to dress up wearing a colorful _____ on her jacket.

B Listening for the Main Ideas

Listen to the story. Answer the following question. Discuss your answer with a partner.

Which of the following best expresses the main idea?

    a. The lady in the pot helped the frog learn to dance.
    b. The frog asked the lady in the pot to dance.
    c. The frog helped the lady in the pot to dream again.

C Listening for Details

Read the following statements. Listen to the story again. Mark the statements T (true) or F (false). Compare your answers with those of another student.

_____ **1.** The lady in the pot was made of painted china.

_____ **2.** She had been a large powder puff.*

*something used to put powder on a woman's face

_____ **3.** The lady in the pot had waltzed* with a handsome prince.

*dance to a slow rhythm of three beats

_____ **4.** She heard a heavy step come down to the basement.

_____ **5.** A frog was placed two feet from her.

_____ **6.** The frog was covered in rhinestones* or holes where rhinestones had been.

*jewels made of glass intended to look like diamonds

_____ **7.** The frog had been a pin.

_____ **8.** The lady asked the frog to play his banjo.

_____ **9.** The lady had to listen to the frog play because she could go nowhere.

_____ **10.** The lady refused to dance with the frog.

D Listening for Inference

The moral of the story is clearly stated in "The Lady in the Pot."
The storyteller says:

> So remember: Never, never, never, never, never give up your dreams
> for they may come to pass* when you least expect them.   *happen

What other morals, or life lessons, might we learn from "The Lady in the Pot"?

Listen to the story again. Work with a partner. Write one or two other morals that the story teaches us. Think about the past life of the lady in the pot. Think about the frog.

1. _____

2. _____

E Discussion

Work in groups. Discuss your answers to the following questions.

1. Why do people sometimes give up their dreams? What happens to them?
2. What dreams have you forgotten? What dreams do you still have?

F Looking at Language

Grammar: Past Perfect Tense

1. *Read the excerpt from the story. Notice the highlighted verbs. Why are different verb tenses used? Which verbs express an earlier time in the past? Which verbs express a later time in the past?*

> Now she **lived** in a small clay pot that hung on a nail in a forgotten corner of the basement. Now when she**'d been** a music box, she **had** always **dreamed** that a handsome prince would come and waltz with her, and together they would go dancing off into the magic world outside.

"The Lady in the Pot" is told in the **simple past.** The first sentence above uses the simple past to describe the situation of the lady in the basement. The second sentence refers to an earlier time, her life before the music box was broken. These verbs are in the **past perfect tense.**

To form the past perfect, use *had* + **past participle.**

Past Perfect	**Simple Past**
	(to describe the time when the story takes place)

-->

She<u>'d been</u> a music box. She <u>had</u> always <u>dreamed</u> . . .	She <u>lived</u> in a small clay pot.

The past perfect tense is only used when we want to contrast two events in the past, when we need to show that one event happened before another event. The events can be put in either order.

> Before she lived in a clay pot, she <u>had been</u> a music box.
> She <u>had been</u> a music box before she lived in a clay pot.

Certain words can signal the contrasting events.

- Words that are used to introduce the first event (past perfect): *after, as soon as.*

  <u>After</u> the lady in the pot <u>had been</u> a music box, she lived in a clay pot.

- Words that are used to introduce the second event (simple past): *before, by the time.*

  <u>Before</u> she <u>lived</u> in a clay pot, the lady in the pot had been a music box.

- *Already, never,* and *ever* are often used with the past perfect to emphasize the event happened first.

  No one <u>had ever asked</u> the lady in the pot to dance before.

2. **Use the events from "The Lady in the Pot" to practice using the past perfect tense. Complete the sentences below. Use the past perfect for the first action. Use the simple past for the second action. The first one has been done for you.**

1. After the lady in the pot **had smashed** (smash) onto the floor, she **lived** (live) in a small clay pot in the basement.

2. Just before the lady in the pot _____ (start) listening to the frog's music, she _____ (tell) the frog to go away.

3. She _____ (live) in a small clay pot in the basement for quite a while by the time a small frog _____ (come) to live in the basement.

4. As soon as the frog _____ (offer) to play music, the lady in the pot _____ (tell) him to go away.

5. The lady in the pot _____ (dream) of a handsome prince before the music box _____ (smash) onto the floor.

6. After the frog _____ (move) into the basement, he _____ (offer) to play music for the lady in the pot.

7. By the time the frog _____ (ask) the lady in the pot to dance, she _____ already _____ (be) carried away by his music.

NOTE: It is also possible to use the simple past for both actions in items 1, 4, and 6.

Ⓐ Synthesis

1. *Work in groups. Consider the three fables in this unit. Which animals are used? What characteristics or features do they possess that help to teach a life lesson?*

	Animal(s)	Characteristics / Features
Fable 1: "The Dove and the Ant"		
Fable 2: "The Prince Who Thought He Was a Rooster"		
Fable 3: "The Lady in the Pot"		

Anthropomorphism suggests that animals or objects have the same feelings and qualities as humans. Fables often use anthropomorphism to teach us life lessons. Animals are the main characters in the story.

One of the most famous fables is "The Tortoise and the Hare." In this story, a slow and steady tortoise (turtle) has a race with a quick and speedy hare (rabbit). The hare is very sure he will win, so he stops to rest during the race. But, in the end, the slow tortoise wins the race because he never stops going. The animals are like different people: quick but lazy; slow but determined.

2. *In which of the three stories is anthropomorphism used? In which of the three stories is anthropomorphism not used, even though there is an animal? Explain.*

B Analysis

Fables are generally written with a problem / solution structure. The characters (often animals) are faced with a problem. They then find a solution to their problem. The solution is usually the life lesson we learn from the story.

Work in groups. Consider the problems and solutions in each story. Take notes. The first problem / solution has been done for you.

	Problems	Solutions
"The Dove and the Ant"	*The ant was in the river and could have drowned.*	*The dove flew down to save him.*
"The Prince Who Thought He Was a Rooster"		
"The Lady in the Pot"		

C Creation

Write a fable. You can write your own fable, or you can retell (in English) a well-known fable from your culture. Try to use language studied in this unit. After editing it, read your fable to the class. Plan your story with the following questions in mind.

1. What moral, or life lesson, will you teach?
2. What is the problem? What is the solution?
3. Who are the characters? Will any animals be used?
4. Consider the sequence of events.

Cooking Tips

Who is the best cook you know? What does this person do to make food special?

Cooking shows have become more and more popular on radio and television. Chefs give tips (helpful suggestions) on how to make new, creative dishes or new ways to prepare foods. They also give tips on cooking popular foods. Some tips even solve cooking problems that people have.

In this unit, you will hear three excerpts from interviews on cooking shows. The excerpts focus on cooking tips by well-known chefs.

LISTENING 1: Chef Larry, from *The Chef Larry Show*, gives tips for preparing a turkey.

LISTENING 2: Russ Parsons gives tips for making a piecrust on Jim Coleman's show *A Chef's Table*.

LISTENING 3: Hugh Carpenter gives tips for cooking steak on a barbecue on the *Gourmet Table* show.

Chef Larry, Jamie, and Eric of *The Chef Larry Show*, a radio talk show in San Diego, California

Work in groups. Discuss your answers to the following questions.

1. Thanksgiving dinner is probably the most important dinner of the year in the United States. It's a time when most families get together and share a meal. When do families in your culture get together and share a meal? What is the holiday? What do they eat at the meal?

2. What special arrangements have to be made for traditional meals in your culture? How much time is spent in preparing for the meal?

Ⓐ Vocabulary Preview

Read the following sentences. Guess the meaning of the underlined words. Then circle a definition or synonym for each word.

1. When buying meat for a dinner for six people, you should <u>figure</u> about one-half pound per person.
   - **a.** cook
   - **b.** estimate
   - **c.** prepare

2. I made too much food for my dinner party last night, but I was happy to have <u>leftovers</u> when I got home late from work tonight.
   - **a.** fresh food
   - **b.** no food
   - **c.** extra food

3. I couldn't make a barbecued chicken dinner because when I got home I realized that my chicken was still <u>frozen</u>.
   - **a.** uncooked
   - **b.** preserved by being kept at a low temperature
   - **c.** not fresh

4. My mother never buys anything at the normal price; she is always looking for a <u>deal</u>.
   a. new product
   b. used item
   c. low price

5. Let's take the meat out of the freezer now, or it will never <u>thaw</u> in time for dinner.
   a. freeze
   b. defrost; unfreeze
   c. melt

6. Many cooks <u>rinse</u> meat before cooking it. They want to first remove any bacteria that may be on it.
   a. wash off
   b. refrigerate
   c. heat

7. Each evening, when Jason returned home from work, he would <u>pat</u> his dog on the head to say hello.
   a. touch lightly
   b. push quickly
   c. hit hard

8. My grandmother never gave us the recipes for her best dishes. But she did give us some <u>hints</u> about how she prepared them.
   a. ideas that help someone guess
   b. clear details
   c. wrong information

9. The <u>roasting</u> time for a turkey is long; a turkey can spend half a day in the oven!
   a. buying
   b. cutting
   c. cooking

B Listening for the Main Ideas

Listen to the interview. Answer the following question. Discuss your answer with a partner.

According to Chef Larry, what are the three most important things to consider when buying a turkey? (Check three answers.)

_____ a. serving a fresh vs. a frozen turkey

_____ b. getting a deal on a turkey

_____ c. thawing under refrigeration

_____ d. roasting the turkey the right amount of time

_____ e. precooking the turkey

C Listening for Details

Listen to the interview again. Match the tips with the correct information. Compare your answers with those of another student.

____ **1.** amount of turkey per person   **a.** 375 degrees

____ **2.** bone weight in bone-in turkey   **b.** 2 1/2 –3 hours

____ **3.** preorder fresh turkey   **c.** 1–2 days before

____ **4.** days to defrost turkey in refrigerator   **d.** 1 pound

____ **5.** cooking time for a 10 to 12 pound turkey   **e.** 4 1/2 hours

____ **6.** temperature for cooking a turkey   **f.** 70%

____ **7.** cooking time for a 16 to 18 pound turkey   **g.** 3 1/2 – 4 1/4 hours

____ **8.** cooking time for a turkey over 20 pounds   **h.** 5–7 days

D Listening for Inference

Listen to the excerpt from the interview. Mark the statements T (true) or F (false). Discuss your answers with a partner.

____ **1.** Each person eats a pound of turkey.

____ **2.** There's a lot of meat on a turkey.

____ **3.** It is important to have extra turkey meat after the meal.

E Discussion

Work in groups. Discuss your answers to the following questions.

1. Based on Chef Larry's advice, would you cook a fresh or frozen turkey?
2. Does modern life make cooking traditional meals more difficult? If so, how?

F Looking at Language

Grammar: Real (Factual) Conditionals

1. *Read the excerpts from the interview. Is the speaker talking about real or unreal possibilities / situations? Notice the highlighted words. What verb tense is used in these examples?*

Excerpt 1

If you **have** a turkey that is over 20 hours, excuse me, 20 pounds (you almost have to cook it 20 hours), you **have to** cook it 4 1/2 hours.

Excerpt 2

. . . if you **precook** it, you **need** nearly the same time to reheat it.

> The preceding sentences are real (factual) conditionals. Factual conditional sentences say what usually happens when a certain condition (situation) exists. They express real possibilities / situations that occur for a particular condition.
>
> Notice that the verb tense used is present tense. Factual conditionals contain an *if* clause and a **main** clause. The *if* clause states the condition; the **main** clause states the result of the condition. *When* can be used instead of *if* in factual conditional sentences. The meaning is the same.
>
> | *If* clause | Main clause |
> | --- | --- |
> | *If* (*When*) + subject + simple present tense, . . . | subject + simple present tense |
> | <u>If a turkey weighs</u> over twenty pounds, . . . | <u>you cook</u> it for 4 1/2 hours. |
> | <u>When you thaw</u> a frozen turkey, . . . | <u>you should leave</u> it in the refrigerator for 5 to 7 days. |

2. Work with a partner.

Student A: You want to buy a fresh turkey. You think the holiday is special, and you want to make a special dinner.
Student B: You want to buy a frozen turkey. You are working late and can't be bothered with a lot of food preparation.

*Convince your partner that your choice is better. Use factual conditionals with the information listed under your turkey. Add your own ideas. For variety, use the following verbs in your conditional (**if**) clauses:*
*If you **buy** / **get** / **purchase** / **choose** / **select** . . .*

Student A	**Student B**
• You can preorder it	• It's sometimes free in supermarkets (after buying $100 of groceries).
• It tastes better	• You don't have to run around for two days.
• You don't have to remember to defrost it	• You can leave it in the refrigerator to defrost.
• _____	• _____
• _____	• _____

Jim Coleman is host of *A Chef's Table,* a radio cooking show in Philadelphia, Pennsylvania. In this excerpt of his show, he interviews another chef, Russ Parsons.

Work in groups. Discuss your answers to the following questions.

1. What popular dish or food do people in your culture find difficult to make? Do people give each other tips on how to make it?

2. Pie is a traditional American dessert. Have you eaten pies? Is pie similar to any desserts in your culture?

Ⓐ Vocabulary Preview

Read the definitions of the following words. Then complete the sentences with the best word.

critical:	fundamental; very important
crust:	the baked outer part of foods such as pies
moistened:	made slightly wet
valid:	acceptable
flaky:	made of light, thin pieces that break easily
restraint:	stopping; holding back
lousy:	very bad
rolling:	moving by turning over and over
smashing:	dropping, throwing, or hitting violently
stretching:	making something bigger by pulling it

1. This pie is delicious! The apples are so sweet, and the _____ is so light!

2. My grandmother always made a short,* heavy piecrust; I preferred my mother's piecrust, which was always light and _____.

*made with a lot of butter or fat

3. _____ pizza dough takes a lot of practice. It's hard to keep it from tearing.

4. My mother is an excellent cook, but I've always been a _____ one.

5. We have to make ten pies for tomorrow's party. We'll be _____ out pie dough all night!

6. The pie dough felt too dry, so he added water until it was well _____.

7. Each time my little brother got angry, he began _____ his toys in his bedroom.

8. Try to show some _____ when using salt in your food. Too much salt is not good for you!

9. Jean never makes dinner for her friends anymore. I guess having three small children is a _____ reason!

10. The most _____ thing in roasting a turkey is the cooking time.

B Listening for the Main Ideas

Listen to the interview. Choose the correct answer. Discuss your answers with a partner.

1. One thing that is *easy* to control when making a piecrust is how you _____.
   a. mix the ingredients   **b.** roll the dough   **c.** bake it

2. One thing that is *more difficult* to learn to control in making a piecrust is how you _____.
   a. mix the ingredients   **b.** roll the dough   **c.** bake it

C Listening for Details

Read the following statements. Listen to the interview again. Mark the statements T (true) or F (false). Compare your answers with those of another student.

____ **1.** Piecrusts are really easy to make.

____ **2.** There is one critical thing about making piecrusts.

____ **3.** You can control how the butter is cut into the flour.

____ **4.** Your piecrust should look like slightly moistened cornmeal.

_____ **5.** A flaky crust is an American crust.

_____ **6.** For a flaky crust, you should leave in chunks of butter.

_____ **7.** Russ Parsons spent an entire summer making piecrusts.

_____ **8.** Today he's a great piecrust maker.

_____ **9.** How you hold your elbows is very important.

_____**10.** You should smash and stretch your piecrust.

_____**11.** When rolling out a piecrust, you should press down on it like an old macho* guy.

*strong, but not sensitive or sympathetic

Ⓓ Listening for Inference

Listen to the excerpts from the interview. Try to understand what Russ Parsons might be saying about the way people make piecrusts. Then answer the following questions. Discuss your answers with a partner.

Excerpt 1

How does Russ Parsons feel about short crusts?

    a. He thinks they are better than flaky crusts.
    b. He thinks they are not as good as flaky crusts.
    c. He thinks they are as good as flaky crusts.

Excerpt 2

What is Russ Parsons saying about someone who smashes the piecrust?

    a. That person is a great crust maker.
    b. That person is an angry crust maker.
    c. That person is not a successful crust maker.

Ⓔ Discussion

Work in groups. Discuss your answers to the following questions.

1. Pie is a traditional American dessert. For many people, pie is a symbol for American life. We hear expressions like "mom's apple pie" or "American pie." However, most Americans say they cannot make a piecrust. Homemade pies are disappearing. Why do you think this is true?
2. What traditional foods are disappearing from your culture because people no longer know how to make them?

F Looking at Language

Pronunciation: Reduced Words

1. *Read the excerpt from the interview as you listen to it. Notice the highlighted words. How are they pronounced in everyday speech?*

> What you're **going to** get is a European-style pastry crust . . . like a tart crust. Uh, it'll be very short. Uh, which is not a . . . that's a perfectly valid type of crust. It's just a short crust. If you **want to** have a flaky crust, which is, you know, the kind of, the American epitome, what you **have to** do is, you have to show some restraint.

In everyday speech, some words are reduced. These are usually function words (articles, helping verbs, short prepositions, personal pronouns, and some conjunctions). If a word is reduced, it connects with the word before it and both words are reduced. In the excerpt above, the word *to* is reduced in all three examples. The words in front of *to* are also reduced.

Written English	Spoken English (how the words sound)
What you're <u>going to</u> get is a European-style pastry crust.	What you're <u>gonna</u> get is a European-style pastry crust.
If you <u>want to</u> have a flaky crust . . .	If you <u>wanna</u> have a flaky crust . . .
What you <u>have to</u> do is . . .	What you <u>hafta</u> do is . . .

Reductions are **not** common in short answers or comments. When the function word is at the end of a sentence, it is usually pronounced fully and not reduced. For example, the full pronunciation is more common in B's response:

A: We <u>hafta</u> go shopping now.

B: Oh, I'm so tired. Do we <u>have to</u>?

2. *Listen to the dialogue. Notice the highlighted phrases. Circle the phrases that are reduced in normal speech. Then work in pairs. Practice reading the dialogue with the correct reductions. Change roles.*

A: You **have to** help me make a dessert this afternoon. We're having guests to dinner tonight.

B: Do I **have to**? I told Hannah I could go to the game with her today.

A: Didn't you say that you **want to** learn how to make a piecrust?

B: Yes, but not today! I'm **going to** miss an important game! Can't I go?

A: If you **want to**. But I'm making a cherry pie with those beautiful cherries we bought yesterday. Have you tasted them yet?

B: No, but I'm **going to**.

A: Here. Try one. Pretty good, aren't they?

B: OK, I'm **going to** stay and help you make dessert!

Work in groups. Discuss your answers to the following questions.

1. Grilling steaks on a barbecue is an American tradition in the summer. Traditionally, men do the grilling. Are there any foods that men usually cook in your culture? If so, what are they?
2. Do you like grilled food? If so, what kind of things do you like grilled?

Ⓐ Vocabulary Preview

Read the following recipe. Guess the meaning of the underlined words. Then match the number of each word with a synonym or definition from page 111.

Barbecued Chicken

Chicken can become dry when cooked on a barbecue. Before grilling, precook chicken pieces in oven to (**1**) seal in the juices.

Set oven (**2**) thermometer at 250 degrees. Cook chicken for 20 minutes. Chicken should be (**3**) medium rare before you grill it on a (**4**) charcoal grill.

Place the chicken pieces on the middle of a hot grill, not too close to the (**5**) edges. (**6**) Sear the chicken pieces to give them black marks from the grill. When the chicken has a good (**7**) char, brush some barbecue sauce over all the pieces. Lower the heat, and cook for 5 minutes. The barbecue sauce will begin to caramelize, or thicken. Then turn the pieces over. Brush the chicken pieces on the other side. Cook for another 5 minutes.

Close the barbecue (**8**) lid slightly. Leave the lid (**9**) cracked open for smoke to get out. Continue to cook the chicken in a low temperature (**10**) environment until done (about 8–10 minutes).

_____ **a.** opened just a little

_____ **b.** partly cooked; pink inside

_____ **c.** something that measures temperature

_____ **d.** cover; top

_____ **e.** black substance made of burned wood; used for grilling food outdoors

_____ **f.** burn with a sudden, powerful heat

_____ **g.** conditions or surroundings

_____ **h.** hold in; keep in

_____ **i.** black burn mark

_____ **j.** parts of something that are farthest from the center

Ⓑ Listening for the Main Ideas

Listen to the interview. Choose the correct answer. Discuss your answers with a partner.

1. When first cooking steak on a grill, start cooking it on _____.
   a. a high heat   **b.** a medium heat   **c.** a low heat

2. After you sear a steak on a grill, it should be kept in a _____ heat environment.
   a. low (300°F)   **b.** high (400°F)   **c.** very high (500°F)

Ⓒ Listening for Details

Read the following questions. Listen to the interview again. Circle the best answer for each question. Compare your answers with those of another student.

1. On which kind of barbecue should you sear a steak?
   a. a gas barbecue   **b.** a charcoal barbecue   **c.** either a gas or charcoal barbecue

2. How do you reduce the heat of the barbecue?
   a. turn off all gas jets   **b.** turn off all gas jets except one   **c.** turn all gas jets to lowest possible settings

3. When should you close the barbecue lid?
   a. when the steaks are red   **b.** when the steaks are charred   **c.** when the steaks are fatty

4. What happens to the barbecue sauce?
   a. It comes off the steak.   **b.** It becomes thicker.   **c.** It loses some of its flavor.

5. How should you cook your steak after closing the lid?
   a. intensely   **b.** indirectly   **c.** on a high heat

6. If you follow Hugh Carpenter's advice, your steak will always be _____.
   a. rare   **b.** medium rare   **c.** evenly cooked

7. What does Hugh Carpenter think you need in order to cook steaks well?
   a. practice   **b.** a good barbecue   **c.** a good thermometer

D Listening for Inference

Listen to the excerpts from the interview. Listen to the speaker's intonation and tone of voice. Choose the best answers. Discuss your answers with a partner.

Excerpt 1

The interviewer _____.
   a. is surprised by this advice
   b. knows this advice
   c. is doubtful about this advice

Excerpt 2

Hugh Carpenter _____.
   a. agrees that practice is necessary
   b. thinks practice could help
   c. doesn't seem concerned about practice

E Discussion

Work in groups. Discuss your answers to the following questions.

1. Do you eat meat? If so, is grilling a good way to cook meat, in your opinion? Do you like it rare, medium rare, medium, or well done?
2. Would you follow Hugh Carpenter's advice for grilling meat?

F Looking at Language

Function: Giving Step-by-Step Instructions

1. *Read the excerpts from the interview as you listen to them. Focus on the highlighted words. How do they help the listener follow the cooking tip? What is the function of these phrases?*

Excerpt 1

That's about a medium heat. It takes about two minutes to do it on each side. **And then** to take the steak and to move it away from the heat . . .

Excerpt 2

They have this nice char from the initial browning, the fat's been rendered out, the barbecue sauce is reduced and caramelized, and it's become more intense in flavor, **but now, from now on**, you're cooking it indirectly over very, very low heat . . .

Excerpt 3

Now I would think you would need to practice that a couple of times to get the cooking time down, to get the doneness that you want . . . to figure out for your grill, OK, to get rare or medium rare, **once I move it away from the direct heat**, I need to do this for how long?

When giving instructions, we often link the steps together. In the examples above, the speaker helps his listener follow the steps. He uses certain phrases to show the next step. These phrases help show the cooking process.

Here are common phrases to give step-by-step instructions:

First of all, you . . .	*Make sure you remember to . . .*
The first thing you need to do is . . .	*Be careful not to . . .*
	Remember to . . .
To begin with, . . .	*Finally, you should . . .*
After that, . . .	*At the end, . . .*
The next thing you do is . . . Then, . . .	
Don't forget to . . .	

---

2. *Take Hugh Carpenter's advice for cooking steak on a barbecue. Link together his advice as step-by-step instructions. There are four main steps to his cooking tips.*

Work in pairs. Give directions to your partner. Use phrases from the list above. Then change roles.

EXAMPLE

First of all, you select a piece of meat 1/2 inch thick or more . . .

Step 1	Select a piece of meat 1/2 inch thick or more.
Step 2	Sear it on each side for 2 minutes. Move it away from the heat. Close the barbecue lid.
Step 3	Keep the temperature at 300 degrees. Crack the lid open (if you can't keep the temperature at 300 degrees).
Step 4	Remove meat at desired doneness.

A **Synthesis**

Listen to the three interviews again. Focus on the tips given by the chefs. Fill in the missing information. Then compare your notes with those of other students. Discuss your answers to the questions on page 115.

Interview	Tips
Roasting a Turkey	Buy _____ per person.
	Consider _____ versus _____ .
	Thaw frozen turkey _____ .
	Pat turkey dry before _____ .
	Roast turkey according to _____ .
	Start preparing turkey _____ .
Making a Piecrust	Leave _____ in the crust.
	Practice making crusts _____ .
	Hold _____ the right way.
	_____ the piecrust . . . don't _____ it.
Grilling a Steak	_____ meat to pick up the pattern of the grill.
	Move steak _____ .
	_____ all gas jets except one.
	Finish cooking at _____ heat.
	Crack _____ open.

1. Which food preparation takes the most time?
2. Which one needs the most practice to learn?
3. Which one is the most unusual (not the way people usually cook)?
4. Which one is most worth trying, in your opinion? Why?

B Analysis

In each listening, a chef gives us a cooking tip for a popular American dish. Most Americans know something about roasting a turkey, making a piecrust, and cooking a steak on a barbecue. These are basics in American cooking. However, these chefs tell us something "new." They give us a secret for success.

Review the transcripts for each cooking tip on pages 161–163. What problem in cooking does the tip try to solve? What solution does a chef give us to solve the problem? Discuss your ideas with other students. Fill in the following chart.

	Problem	Solution
Listening 1: Roasting a Turkey		
Listening 2: Making a Piecrust		
Listening 3: Grilling a Steak		

C Creation

Work in pairs. With your partner, write a cooking tip for something you (or a friend or someone in your family) can cook well. Use the chart on page 116 to prepare the steps for your tip. Use language from the Looking at Language sections in this unit.

Include new information about this food preparation. What problem do people sometimes have preparing this dish? What solution can you offer? Give tips.

Tip: How to _____

	Step-by-Step Phrase	Instruction	Special Tip(s)
Step 1			
Step 2			
Step 3			
Step 4			

Women and War

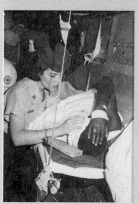

Do women serve in the military in your country? If so, what do they do?

An oral history is an interview in which someone talks about his or her life. An interviewer asks many questions to help a person remember specific situations and events. The person recalls memories of the past; these memories can often be emotional.

In this unit, you will listen to excerpts from three women's oral histories. You will hear about the memories of women who were involved in the Vietnam War, World War II, and the Persian Gulf War. Their experiences were quite different because they experienced war at different times in American history. But they share certain feelings about the difficulty of war.

LISTENING 1: Jeanne Markle on her experience during the Vietnam War

LISTENING 2: Marion Gurfein on her experience during World War II

LISTENING 3: Tomika Perdomo on her experience during the Persian Gulf War

Jeanne Markle, an American nurse who served in the Vietnam War, here with her husband

Work in groups. Discuss your answers to the following questions.

1. What do you know about the Vietnam War? Who fought in this war? What happened?
2. What role do you think women had in the Vietnam War?

Ⓐ Vocabulary Preview

Read the following paragraphs. Guess the meaning of the underlined words. Then match the number of each word with a definition or synonym from below and page 119.

When soldiers return from war, it is not always easy to come home. In some wars, the census (body count of dead soldiers) is very high. Or many physically (**1**) <u>injured</u> soldiers must be cared for. These soldiers may return home without legs or arms. Some may be deaf or (**2**) <u>blind</u>, having lost their hearing or eyesight in battle.

Even worse, these (**3**) <u>veterans</u> must (**4**) <u>face</u> a difficult emotional life when they start their lives again at home. They take off their (**5**) <u>uniforms</u> and put them away. They have to return to (**6**) <u>civilian</u> life and wear civilian clothes again. They might look like other people, but they don't feel like other people. They are often (**7**) <u>depressed</u> by what they have seen in war. Often their feelings are (**8**) <u>bottled up</u> inside because they don't want to talk about their war experiences. They may think people at home cannot understand their war experiences. They may even miss being in the war because it was a place where they were (**9**) <u>appreciated</u> by the people around them. The other soldiers who were fighting beside them understood what they were feeling.

_____ **a.** unexpressed; held inside

_____ **b.** respected; valued

_____ **c.** hurt

____**d.** unable to see

____**e.** related to a person who is *not* in the military

____**f.** deal with

____**g.** special clothes (for example, worn by soldiers, nurses, chefs)

____**h.** soldiers who return home from war

____**i.** very sad

B Listening for the Main Ideas

Listen to the oral history. Answer the following questions. Discuss your answers with a partner.

1. What did Jeanne Markle do in Vietnam?
   a. She was a nurse.
   b. She was a soldier.
   c. She was a cook.

2. How did people in her community react to her when she came home?
   a. They wanted to know more about her.
   b. They gave her a homecoming party.
   c. They didn't appreciate her.

C Listening for Details

Read the following questions. Listen to the oral history again. Circle the best answer for each question. Compare your answers with those of another student.

1. How many days a week did Jeanne normally work?
   a. 5
   b. 6
   c. 7

2. Why was Jeanne flying home and leaving her husband, Brian, behind?
   a. She was divorcing her husband.
   b. She was going to have a baby.
   c. She was caring for the injured soldiers on the plane.

3. Why did Jeanne feel depressed in the airplane?
   a. She was going home.
   b. She had to keep caring for injured soldiers.
   c. She thought about her work as a nurse in the war.

4. What was wrong with the blond-headed young man?
   a. He couldn't see.
   b. He couldn't walk.
   c. He couldn't eat.

5. How did the Air Force nurse help him?
   a. She sat with him.
   b. She fed him with a spoon.
   c. She cried with him.

6. What did Jeanne wear going home?
   a. a nurse's uniform
   b. civilian clothes
   c. farming clothes

7. How did Jeanne react when she knew she wasn't appreciated at home?
   a. She started to demonstrate against the war.
   b. She left her farming community.
   c. She kept her emotions bottled up.

D Listening for Inference

Read the following statements. Listen to the oral history again. Mark the statements T (true) or F (false). Discuss your answers with a partner.

_____ **1.** Jeanne had a difficult time leaving her husband behind.

_____ **2.** Jeanne wanted to care for the soldiers on the plane home.

_____ **3.** Jeanne was sure that the blond-headed young man would have a good life.

_____ **4.** A soldier in uniform was not appreciated in America after the Vietnam War.

_____ **5.** Second World War veterans got a better homecoming than Vietnam veterans.

_____ **6.** People in northern Indiana were happy to see Jeanne when she got home.

_____ **7.** Jeanne regretted her work in Vietnam.

E Discussion

Work in groups. Discuss your answers to the following questions.

1. Why wasn't Jeanne given a good homecoming? Why weren't Vietnam veterans accepted when they came home?
2. If you were a nurse, would you volunteer to go to war? Why or why not?

F Looking at Language

Pronunciation: *-ed* **Endings**

1. *Read the sentence from the oral history as you listen to it. Notice the pronunciation of the verb* **worked.** *Does the past tense ending* **-ed** *have the sound /t/, /əd/, or /ɪd/?*

And sometimes you even **worked** on your day off if the census was very high.

If the verb ends in a voiceless consonant sound (but not /t/), the past tense ending is pronounced as /t/.	stop → stopped like → liked	miss → missed finish → finished
If the verb ends in a vowel or a voiced consonant sound (but not /d/), the past tense ending is pronounced as /d/.	call → called return → returned	die → died love → loved
If the verb ends in /t/ or /d/, the past tense ending is pronounced as /ɪd/or /əd/. An extra syllable is added to the verb with this ending.	visit → visited land → landed	appreciate → appreciated decide → decided

In English, the past tense ending or participle forms of regular verbs have three pronunciations: /t/, /d/, and /əd/ or /ɪd/. The pronunciation of -ed depends on the sound before the ending:

2. *Listen to the following sentences from Jeanne Markle's oral history. Listen to the pronunciation of the -ed ending of each underlined word. Some of the examples are past tense verbs. Some of the examples are adjectives (past participles). Write the words in the correct category in the chart below.*

1. We got a lot of <u>injured</u>.
2. And so I was pretty <u>depressed</u> on the trip home.
3. Right across from me there was a blond-<u>headed</u> young man—couldn't have been more than 20—and he had lost both arms and he was also blind.
4. And I <u>watched</u> her try to touch his cheek with the spoon so he could turn that way like a new baby to learn to eat again.
5. I <u>faced</u> people all along the way of my homecoming that didn't want to even know where I came from or what I'd been doing.
6. And we had <u>lived</u> through news bulletins and all the demonstrations.
7. We knew that we weren't <u>appreciated</u> at all.
8. I even came home to Indiana to a small farming community of 400 people in northern Indiana, and they were glad to say "hi" to me, but they didn't ask me anything, and so it all <u>bottled</u> up inside of me for many, many years.

/t/	/d/	/ɪd/

Marion Gurfein, wife of a World War II soldier

Work in groups. Discuss your answers to the following questions.

1. What happens to wives when their husbands have to go to war?
2. What happens to families when husbands come back from war?

Ⓐ Vocabulary Preview

Read the following sentences. Guess the meaning of the underlined words. Then choose a definition or synonym for each word.

1. The soldier's wife was <u>going crazy</u> because she hadn't heard from her husband in months.
   a. getting sick   **b.** feeling happy   **c.** becoming very worried

2. Sarah's hands were <u>trembling</u> as she opened the letter with news of her missing husband.
   a. not moving   **b.** shaking   **c.** closing tightly

3. During World War II, the <u>telegram</u> was the main source of communication.
   a. e-mail   **b.** cable message   **c.** telephone

4. Many families never heard from their sons again after World War II ended. The government considered these men to be people who were missing-in-action.
   a. had been killed in battle   b. had been injured in battle   c. had disappeared in battle

5. It is difficult for families to get in touch with their loved ones who are fighting in a war. Sometimes months go by before they receive any news.
   a. contact   b. forget   c. feel

6. Joe had always wanted to serve his country, but when he was called to go to war, it was a scary experience and he felt very nervous.
   a. happy   b. frightening   c. disappointing

B Listening for the Main Ideas

Listen to the oral history. Answer the following questions. Discuss your answers with a partner.

1. What was one of the greatest moments of Marion's life?
   a. the day Joe came home from the war
   b. the day she met Joe's parents
   c. the day she had her baby

2. What kind of life did Marion have during the war?
   a. She spent nice days in the park.
   b. She had no friends.
   c. She felt scared much of the time.

C Listening for Details

Read the following sentences. Listen to the oral history again. Find and correct the errors in each sentence. Compare your answers with those of a partner.

1. Joe came home for three weeks.

2. Marion waited almost 30 days for her husband.

3. Joe's sisters were up in the living room waiting for him to come home.

4. Marion met Joe at the door to the apartment, and they fell into each other's arms.

5. She took him back and presented him with a beautiful baby boy.

6. Marion was living in a world of men.

7. Marion knew what to say when a "missing-in-action" telegram arrived.

8. Marion sometimes said, "Maybe they will never find him again."

D Listening for Inference

 Listen to the excerpts of Marion's oral history. Focus on her feelings and answer the questions. Discuss your answers with a partner.

Excerpt 1

What word best describes Marion's feelings?

a. crazy
b. happy
c. uncomfortable

Excerpt 2

What word best describes Marion's feelings?

a. crazy
b. happy
c. uncomfortable

E Discussion

Work in groups. Discuss your answers to the following questions.

1. In your opinion, what was the hardest part of Marion's experience?
2. Marion's experience was during World War II. How is war experience different for husbands and wives today?

F Looking at Language

Functional Language: Involving Your Listener

1. *Read the excerpt from Marion's oral history as you listen to it. Notice the highlighted words. Why does she include these words in her questions? How do these phrases affect her questions?*

> **Can you believe** what it was like in 1945? **You know**, how the girls are going crazy because their husbands are gone a few months?

In the above excerpt, the speaker involves the listener in her story. By using the pronoun *you*, she makes her listener feel part of what she says.

The following phrases can involve a listener in a story:

Can you believe . . . ?

You know . . .

If you remember . . .

When you consider that . . .

And what do you think . . . ?

And then do you know what . . . ?

Don't you think . . . ?

I'm sure you would agree that . . .

Do you know what I mean . . . ?

You see . . .

2. *Take two minutes to prepare a few notes about something that happened to you recently. Where were you? Who were you with? What happened?*

Then work in pairs. Student A tells a very short story about what happened, using several phrases from the preceding list to involve the listener. Student B listens and asks questions if necessary, and counts how many such phases are used. Then change roles.

LISTENING 3 | TOMIKA PERDOMO

Tomika Perdomo, U.S. Marine in the Persian Gulf War

Work in groups. Discuss your answers to the following questions.

1. Do you think women should serve in the military? Should they fight as men do?

2. Should women be given special duties if they volunteer to serve? If so, what might they be?

Ⓐ Vocabulary Preview

Read the definitions of the following words and phrases. Then complete the sentences with the best word or phrase.

contract: legal written agreement

distraction: something that takes your attention
                         away from what you are doing

counterparts: people who have the same job as
                         someone else in a different place

gender: being male or female

option: choice

processed out of: officially made to leave

reach out for: take into one's hands or arms

bittersweet: sad and happy at the same time

1. Going to war is a difficult _____ to choose if a woman has small children at home.

2. As soon as she returned home from the war, she and her children ran to _____ each other.

3. Although men and women fight in war side by side, there are important _____ differences between male and female soldiers.

4. When the soldier did not arrive for duty, he was _____ the army.

5. Having children at home can be a big _____ for a soldier fighting a war.

6. Coming home from war can be a(n) _____ experience for many soldiers. They are happy to return to their families, but they may miss doing an important job with other soldiers.

7. In World War II, the American soldiers fought hard to win the war. Their Japanese _____ fought hard as well.

8. Before an American soldier goes to fight in a war, he or she has to sign a _____ with the U.S. government.

Ⓑ Listening for the Main Ideas

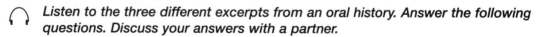

Listen to the three different excerpts from an oral history. Answer the following questions. Discuss your answers with a partner.

1. Tomika talks about leaving her baby home when she went to war. For her, what was the hardest part of being in the Marine Corps?
   a. not hearing from the people at home
   b. working with male soldiers
   c. fighting in the Marine Corps

2. Tomika had to make a difficult decision about going to war. Who did she talk with?

   a. her mother

   b. her friend

   c. her whole family

3. Tomika finally came home. How did her baby react when he saw his mother?

   a. He pushed her away.

   b. He reached out for her.

   c. He held on to her friend, Maxine.

C Listening for Details

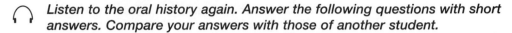

Listen to the oral history again. Answer the following questions with short answers. Compare your answers with those of another student.

1. In the military, who thought hearing from family was a distraction?

2. What is the "gender thing"? How are men and women different when they serve in war, according to Tomika?

3. What would the Marine Corps have done to Tomika if she had chosen *not* to go to war?

4. What advice did Tomika's mother give her?

5. When Tomika first saw her son, how did he look?

6. How did the four-month separation feel to Tomika?

7. What was Tomika's response to her baby holding on to Maxine?

8. How does Tomika define the experience of coming home from war?

D Listening for Inference

Listen to the excerpts from the oral history. Work with a partner. Discuss your answers to the following questions.

Excerpt 1

How does Tomika feel about the men's attitude? Why do you think so?

Excerpt 2

What relationship does Tomika have with her mother? How do you know?

Excerpt 3

What does Tomika mean when she says "I understood"? What did she understand? Did she understand?

E Discussion

Work in groups. Discuss your answers to the following questions.

1. Tomika is a single mom, and she has to leave her baby behind to do her job. What do you think about her decision?

2. Will there be more or fewer women soldiers in the future? Why do you think so?

F Looking at Language

Grammar: Direct or Quoted Speech

🎧 **1.** *Read the following sentences from Tomika's oral history as you listen. Underline the parts that show a speaker's actual words. Where does Tomika quote someone else or herself as she tells her story? How are the sentences punctuated?*

1. And her words were basically, "Did you sign the paper? Did you sign the contract, Tomika?"

2. I said, "Yes ma'am," and she said, "Well, you know what you have to do then."

3. And I looked at him, I'm thinking, "Wow, Maxine, what have you been feeding my son?" . . . you know?

4. So, I reached out for him, he was in her arms, and he kind of looked at me like, "God, I think I know this lady," but he didn't come to me immediately.

When we hear quoted speech, the speaker's voice changes to show that he or she is using someone's exact words. In writing, however, the exact words of a speaker are marked between quotation marks (". . .") and separated by commas. Quoted speech is also called direct speech.

Rules for Writing Direct or Quoted Speech

1. Use a comma after *said*.	*Tomika said, "Yes, ma'am."*
2. Use quotation marks at the beginning and end of the sentence or question.	*Her mother asked, "Did you sign the contract?"*
3. Capitalize the first word in the quotation.	
4. End the quoted speech with a period or question mark.	
5. If direct speech is separated, use a comma before the first quotation mark.	*"Yes ma'am," she said. "I signed the contract."*
6. The second quote begins with a new quotation mark and a capital letter if there is a new sentence. The second quote begins with a lowercase letter if it finishes the first sentence.	*"He was so big," Tomika said, "and he looked so good."*

🎧 **2.** *Listen to the following sentences. Notice the speaker's change of voice when quoting a speaker's actual words. Punctuate the sentences with quotes, commas, and capitalization according to the rules above.*

1. Tomika said I needed to hear their voices

2. Tomika said that's when the gender thing comes in

3. My male counterparts said Tomika knew that their wives at home were taking care of things

4. Tomika said if I did not go I had to face the choice of being processed out of the Marine Corps very hard decision for me at the time

5. Tomika's mother asked did you sign the paper did you sign the contract Tomika

6. Tomika's mother said then you know what you have to do

7. Tomika asked Maxine what have you been feeding my son

8. Even though four months is a short time Tomika said it was a pretty long time to not be with your mom

9. Tomika said wow whew

10. It really kind of hurt Tomika said but I understood

3. *Now work in pairs. Read the statements. Practice changing your voice to indicate direct speech.*

WRAP UP

Ⓐ Synthesis

Differences

You have heard three different women tell their stories. Each story represents typical roles of women at different times in American history. Match the woman's name with her role.

Jeanne Markle, Vietnam War	A soldier going to war
Marion Gurfein, World War II	A nurse caring for injured soldiers
Tomika Perdomo, Persian Gulf War	A wife waiting for a husband to come home

Which role do you think was the most difficult for women? Discuss your answers with other students.

Similarities

Although their stories are different, the women share many war experiences. Check (✓) the woman's name if she had the experience. Discuss your answers in groups.

	Jeanne	Marion	Tomika
Separation from husband or wife			
Death in war			
Separation from baby			
Difficult homecoming			
Worry because of no news			

B Analysis

A good oral history comes from a good interview. An interviewer must ask good questions to help the interviewee remember his or her past experiences and feelings.

Read the following excerpts from the women's oral histories. Put yourself in the place of the interviewer. Imagine what question could have been asked to produce the woman's comment. Circle a, b, or c. Discuss your choices with another student.

Jeanne Markle

They were 12-hour shifts a day and six days a week. And sometimes you even worked on your day off if the census was very high. And the helicopters after we opened came in all the time every day. It was a busy hospital. We got a lot of injured.

a. Interviewer: Describe your work as a nurse in Vietnam.
b. Interviewer: Why were you sent to Vietnam?
c. Interviewer: Were there many injured soldiers?

Marion Gurfein

So, we were all up in the living room sitting there. Joe's parents, my mother, my sisters. And I heard the elevator come up. Look at me, I'm still trembling. And I ran out into the hall and ran over to the elevator and the door opened and there was Joe, and I guess that was one of the greatest moments of my life. I mean, we fell into each other's arms. And I can't remember exactly what we said, but took him back and presented him with this beautiful little girl.

a. Interviewer: Describe the years you waited for your husband to return home.
b. Interviewer: What was it like to raise a family without your husband at home?
c. Interviewer: Describe your husband's homecoming.

Tomika Perdomo

Because as a single parent, they gave me the option to either go or not to go. If I went, of course I had to have someone watch him. If I did not go, I had to face the choice of being processed out of the Marine Corps. Very hard decision for me at the time, so I called my mother so she could help me out a little bit. And her words were basically, "Did you sign the paper? Did you sign the contract, Tomika?" I said, "Yes ma'am," and she said, "Well, then you know what you have to do then."

a. Interviewer: How difficult was it for you to be away from your family?
b. Interviewer: How did you decide to go to the Persian Gulf War?
c. Interviewer: What were your duties in the Persian Gulf War?

ⓒ Creation

Work in pairs. Conduct an oral history. Follow the instructions.

1. Prepare your questions. Use the outline and the following cues to write your questions. Some examples are provided for you.

I. War Experiences

A. War: *Which war did you experience?*

B. Place:

C. Length of stay:

D. Job / Position:

E. Most memorable wartime experience:

II. Life Experiences during War

    A. Family contact: *Did you have contact with your family?*

    B. Food:

    C. Friends:

    D. Entertainment:

    E. Emotional situation:

III. Coming Home

    A. Where: *Did you return home after the war? Where did you go?*

    B. New activities (work? school?):

    C. People's attitudes at home:

    D. Feelings about being home:

2. Find a person who has experienced war, and conduct a short interview. (If you cannot find a person who has lived through a war, interview someone who has a friend or relative who has experienced war.) You may interview someone together, or you may each conduct separate interviews.

3. Present your oral histories in class. Compare and contrast the experiences of the people you interviewed.

Genre: POETRY

Do you enjoy reading poetry? Do you have a favorite poem? What is it?

Poetry is a form of expression that has been popular through the ages. The themes in poetry often deal with love, death, nature and the seasons, or sometimes just daily life. The vocabulary in poetry is often very descriptive; it is sometimes uncommon.

In this unit, you will listen to three famous American poets reading their own work.

LISTENING 1: "Stopping by Woods on a Snowy Evening" by Robert Frost

LISTENING 2: "When faces called flowers float out of the ground" by e.e. cummings

LISTENING 3: "Late October" by Maya Angelou

Robert Frost lived from 1874 to 1963. His work is known for its settings in New England. You will listen to him read "Stopping by Woods on a Snowy Evening."

Work in groups. Discuss your answers to the following questions.

1. What is special about the winter season?
2. Which adjectives best describe winter in your opinion? Make a list.

Ⓐ Vocabulary Preview

Read the definitions of the following words. Then complete the sentences with the best word.

woods:	an area of land covered with trees
queer:	strange (an old-fashioned use)
harness:	set of leather bands fastened with metal, usually used to control a horse and attach it to a vehicle that it pulls
shake:	move up and down or from side to side with quick movements
sweep:	a quick, forceful movement
downy:	having the quality of thin, soft feathers
flake:	a very small, thin piece of something (like chocolate or snow)

1. Jack is very excited. He just saw the first snow _____, which means that winter is coming.

2. It feels comfortable here now, but when the _____ of wind comes through this house, you will feel cold.

3. When we were young, my brother and I would take long walks and sometimes get lost in the _____.

4. My dog's behavior is very _____ today. He won't eat or drink, and he's walking around the house in circles!

5. The horse has a _____. Let's attach the wagon and go for a ride!

6. I'm not sure if there is any water in that bottle. _____ it to see if there's any left.

7. Everyone wanted to touch the baby's soft, _____ hair.

Ⓑ Listening for the Main Ideas

Listen to the poem. Answer the following questions. Discuss your answers with a partner.

1. Why does the poet stop in the woods?
   a. To visit a man who lives there.
   b. To watch the woods fill up with snow.
   c. To let his horse drink from the lake.

2. Why doesn't the poet stop for a long time to look at the woods?
   a. He needs to get to the village.
   b. There is too much snow.
   c. He still has miles to travel.

Ⓒ Listening for Details

Read the following questions. Listen to the poem again. Circle the best answer for each question. Compare your answers with those of another student.

1. The poet knows the man who owns the woods. Where is the man's house?
   a. in the woods   **b.** in the village

2. What does the poet say about this man?
   a. He won't see the poet stop.   **b.** He will see the poet stop.

3. How does the horse react to being in the woods?
   a. He wants to stop in the woods.   **b.** He doesn't want to stop in the woods.

4. What kind of evening is it?
   a. frozen   **b.** dark

5. How does the horse show that he is confused?
   a. He shakes the bells on his harness.   **b.** He refuses to stop.

6. What sound does the poet hear?
   a. someone walking   **b.** the sweep of the wind

7. How does the poet describe the woods?
   a. lovely and bright   **b.** dark and deep

8. What does the poet need to do?
   a. keep promises   **b.** go to sleep

D Listening for Inference

Poetry can be read on two different levels: literal (basic or ordinary) and figurative (what you imagine the poet means; different from the literal meaning). In Section C above, you focused on the literal details of the poem. Now consider the figurative meaning of the last four lines of the poem.

Read the last four lines of the poem as you listen to them. Then work with a partner to answer the question below.

> The woods are lovely, dark, and deep,
>
> But I have promises to keep,
>
> And miles to go before I sleep,
>
> And miles to go before I sleep.

What is the poet saying? Think of possible interpretations for *woods*, *promises*, and *sleep*.

Write your interpretation.

The poet is saying that _____

_____

E Discussion

Work in groups. Discuss your answers to the following questions.

1. This is one of Robert Frost's most popular poems. Why do you think it is so popular?
2. Do you like the poem? Why or why not?

F Looking at Language

Pronunciation: Prepositions

1. *Read the poem as you listen to it. Focus on the highlighted phrases. What do you notice about the pronunciation of the prepositions in these phrases? Which ones are stressed? Which ones are not stressed?*

> Whose woods these are I think I know.
> His house is **in the village**, though;
> He will not see me stopping here
> To watch his woods fill up **with snow**.
>
> My little horse must think it queer
> To stop without a farmhouse near
> Between the woods and frozen lake
> The darkest evening **of the year**.
>
> He gives his harness bells a shake
> To ask if there is some mistake.
> The only other sound's the sweep
> **Of easy wind and downy flake**.

The woods are lovely, dark, and deep,
But I have promises to keep,
And miles to go **before I sleep**,
And miles to go **before I sleep**.

In English, short prepositions are generally not stressed in everyday speech. They are pronounced with a reduced vowel.

In the preceding examples, the prepositions *without*, *between*, and *before* are not short. They are not reduced. However, the prepositions *in*, *with*, and *of* have reduced sounds.

Preposition	Pronunciation in everyday speech
in	/ən/
with	/wɪt/
of	/əv/

NOTE: In the preceding poem, there are additional phrases, *to watch*, *to stop*, *to ask*, and *to keep*. These phrases are infinitives of purpose. The word *to* is reduced to /tə/, except when it appears before a vowel. So, in the phrase *to ask*, *to* is pronounced /tuw/.

---

2. *Work in pairs. Student A asks questions 1–4. Student B chooses the correct answer from the list. Then Student B asks questions 5–8 and Student A answers. Remember to use reductions when necessary.*

Student A	**Student B**
1. Where does the poet take his horse?	In the village
2. Where is the man's house?	At a lake
3. Where does the poet stop with his horse?	To the woods
4. Why does the poet stop in the woods?	For a rest

Student B	**Student A**
5. Why does the horse shake his harness?	On the horse
6. Where is the harness?	In the wind
7. Where is the sweeping sound heard?	For miles
8. How much farther must the poet travel?	To ask if there's a mistake

by e. e. cummings

e. e. cummings (he often used lowercase letters in his poems, as well as in his name) lived from 1894 to 1962. His work is known for its playful language. You will listen to him read "when faces called flowers float out of the ground."

Work in groups. Discuss your answers to the following questions.

1. What is special about the spring season?

2. Which adjectives best describe spring in your opinion? Make a list.

Ⓐ Vocabulary Preview

Read the following sentences. Guess the meaning of the underlined words. Then match each word with the letter of a definition or synonym from page 139.

____ **1.** I love to look up at the sky and watch the clouds <u>float</u> by!

____ **2.** Josh's <u>doubting</u> bothers me; he never believes anything anyone tells him!

____ **3.** My favorite memory of the farm was watching the young horses <u>frolic</u> with their mother.

____ **4.** My Aunt Tillie is a <u>spry</u> 80-year-old who never misses a chance to go dancing!

____ **5.** My parents did not like my grandmother's <u>doting</u> on me. They thought she spoiled me with all her kisses and cookies!

____ **6.** My father thought the politician's ideas were <u>nonsense</u> and that he shouldn't be elected.

____ **7.** Every morning, Matt would <u>hover</u> by the door, hoping to talk to me.

____ **8.** My dog <u>quivers</u> with excitement whenever I give her a bone.

____ **9.** The cat, <u>cringing</u> with fear, climbed up the tree away from the barking dog.

a. ideas, statements, or opinions that are not true or that seem very stupid

b. stay up in the air without sinking

c. moving back or away from someone or something because you are afraid

d. loving and caring about someone more than people think you should

e. shakes slightly

f. active and cheerful (but old)

g. play in an active, happy way

h. stay around one place, especially because you are waiting for something

i. thinking that things are untrue or unlikely

B Listening for the Main Ideas

Listen to the poem. Answer the following question. Discuss your answer with a partner.

Which of the following best expresses the main idea of the poem?

a. being alive and enjoying the moment

b. the importance of keeping things such as memories

c. the spirit of giving things to people who need them

C Listening for Details

Read the following words from the poem. Some of the words refer to the poet's view of spring. Other words do not represent the poet's view of spring. Listen to the poem again. As you listen, write the letter of each word in the correct box.

The poet's view of spring	Not the poet's view of spring

a. wishing

b. keeping

c. doubting

d. frolic

e. dancing

f. giving

g. doting

h. nonsense

i. alive

j. quiver

k. cringing

l. night

D Listening for Inference

Work with a partner. Read the excerpts from the poem as you listen to them and answer the following questions.

1. Focus on the rhyme (words that end in the same sounds). Do the words in a line sound the same, or do they sound different? Which line has more rhyme? Which line sounds more positive? Which line sounds more negative?

2. Focus on intonation (the way the poet's voice changes). Does the intonation rise (go up) or fall (go down)? Which line has a rising intonation? Which line has a falling intonation? Which line sounds more positive? Which line sounds more negative?

3. How do rhyme and intonation affect the poet's meaning? How is the meaning in each of the 2 lines different?

Excerpt 1

and breathing is wishing and wishing is having—
but keeping is downward and doubting and never

Excerpt 2

and wishing is having and having is giving—
but keeping is doting and nothing and nonsense

Excerpt 3

and having is giving and giving is living—
but keeping is darkness and winter and cringing

E Discussion

Work in groups. Discuss your answers to the following questions.

1. Do you have the same feelings about spring as e. e. cummings? If so, give examples from his poem that express your feelings in spring.

2. Cummings uses many gerunds (-*ing* nouns) to describe spring. For example, *wishing* is a gerund that expresses desire for something new. How would you describe the other seasons with gerunds? Make a list of gerunds for the other three seasons: summer, fall, and winter. (For example, fall could be described by the gerund *dying*.)

F Looking at Language

Grammar: Gerunds

1. *Read the first stanza of the poem. Notice how the highlighted* -ing *words function in the text. There are six nouns and one verb. Which words are nouns? Which word is a verb?*

when faces called flowers float out of the ground
and **breathing** is **wishing** and **wishing** is **having**—
but **keeping** is downward and **doubting** and never
—it's april (yes, april; my darling) it's spring!
yes the pretty birds frolic as spry as can fly
yes the little fish gambol as glad as can be
(yes the mountains are **dancing** together)

Gerunds are verbs that function like nouns. In the examples above, the first six highlighted words are gerunds (nouns). They are subjects and subject complements. Only *dancing* is a verb. The present progressive tense of the verb *dance* describes what the mountains are doing.

- To form a gerund, we use base form of verb + *-ing*.

- To form a negative gerund, we use *not* + base form of verb + *-ing*. Notice that the gerund is always singular and is followed by the third person singular form of the verb, such as *is* in the preceding examples.

2. *In English, certain verbs are following by gerunds. Work in pairs. Take turns asking questions about spring. Use the correct gerund form. You can correct each other's use of gerunds by checking the questions in parentheses.*

   Student A, look at the questions below. Student B, look at page 148.

Student A

1. What do you enjoy _____ (eat) in the spring?

   Answer: _____

2. *(Partner's question: Is there anything you mind doing in the spring?)*

3. What do you avoid _____ (buy) in the spring?

   Answer: _____

4. *(Partner's question: Where do you suggest going during spring vacation?)*

5. What did you regret _____ (do) last spring?

   Answer: _____

6. *(Partner's question: What will you consider doing next spring?)*

7. Where can you imagine _____ (be) in the spring?

   Answer: _____

8. *(Partner's question: What did you quit doing last spring?)*

9. What do you miss _____ (do) in the spring?

   Answer: _____

10. *(Partner's question: What do you like seeing every spring?)*

Maya Angelou was born on April 4, 1928, and currently reads her work around the country. You will listen to her read "Late October."

Work in groups. Discuss your answers to the following questions.

1. What is special about the fall season?
2. Which adjectives best describe fall in your opinion? Make a list.

Ⓐ Vocabulary Preview

1. *This poem has several uncommon words, but it is short and beautiful. For this poem, you will be given some extra help in understanding the language. Begin by underlining all the words that you do not know in the poem. Then, work with another student to see if, together, you can guess the meaning of any of the words you underlined.*

"Late October"
by Maya Angelou

    Carefully
    the leaves of autumn
    sprinkle down the tinny
    sound of little dyings
    and skies sated of ruddy sunsets
    of roseate dawns
    roil ceaselessly in
    cobweb greys and turn
    to black
    for comfort.

    Only lovers
    see the fall
    a signal end to endings

a gruffish gesture alerting
those who will not be alarmed
that we begin to stop
in order simply
to begin
again.

2. Now match these vocabulary words with a definition or synonym. If necessary, use your dictionary for help.

____ **1.** sprinkle   **a.** without stopping

____ **2.** tinny   **b.** with more than enough

____ **3.** sated   **c.** movement with head, arm, or hand that shows
____ **4.** ruddy   what you mean

____ **5.** roseate   **d.** pink

____ **6.** dawn   **e.** time of day when light first appears

____ **7.** roil   **f.** red

____ **8.** ceaselessly   **g.** rain lightly

____ **9.** cobweb   **h.** making someone notice something important

___ **10.** gruffish   **i.** anxious; worried

___ **11.** gesture   **j.** networks of sticky threads made by spiders in order
___ **12.** alerting   to catch insects

___ **13.** alarmed   **k.** like something made of metal

                              l. move

                              m. kind of rough, annoying

Ⓑ Listening for the Main Ideas

Listen to the poem. Don't worry about understanding every word. Listen for the general meaning of the poem. Answer the following question. Discuss your answer with a partner.

Which of the following best expresses the main idea of the poem?

    a. the ending of a season
    b. the ending of sunsets
    c. the ending of love

C Listening for Details

Read the poem on pages 142–143, and listen to it again. Answer the following questions with short answers. Compare your answers with those of another student.

1. What do the leaves sound like?
2. What do the skies look like?
3. What color does the sky turn?
4. What kind of gesture is the fall to lovers?
5. Why do we begin to stop?

D Listening for Inference

Read the second stanza of the poem as you listen to it. What do you think the poet is saying about lovers in the fall? Choose the best answers. Discuss your answers with a partner.

> Only lovers
> see the fall
> a signal end to endings
> a gruffish gesture alerting
> those who will not be alarmed
> that we begin to stop
> in order simply
> to begin
> again.

1. How do lovers see the fall?
   a. as the end
   b. as a new beginning
2. How do others (those who will not be alarmed) see the fall?
   a. as the end
   b. as a new beginning

E Discussion

Work in groups. Discuss your answers to the following questions.

1. How does the poet feel about late October? Is this a happy poem or a sad poem? Why?
2. How do you feel in the fall? Is it a happy or sad time for you? Do you feel differently in the fall than in other seasons?

F Looking at Language

Function: Using Metaphor

1. *Read the following lines from the poem. What is unusual about the highlighted words in this context? Is this a normal usage of these words? Why does the poet use these words here?*

the leaves of autumn **sprinkle** down . . .
skies . . . roil ceaselessly . . . in **cobweb** greys . . .

> Metaphor is common in poetry. Metaphor is a way of describing something by comparing it to something else that has similar qualities without using *like* or *as*.
>
> In the examples above, *sprinkle* gives a special meaning to falling leaves. Leaves do not usually sprinkle. Rain does. But the verb *sprinkle* creates an interesting picture of leaves falling, like the rain does. *Cobweb* gives a special meaning to the color grey. We do not usually use *cobweb* to describe color, although cobwebs are dark or grey in color. As a metaphor, *cobweb* gives a special quality to the color grey.

2. *Work in small groups. Read the following sentences. They each use common metaphors. Try to identify the comparison that is made in each case. Explain the unusual use of the underlined words. Then compare your answers with the answers of another group.*

1. I don't want to spend time calling all those people. <u>Time is money</u>!
2. His girlfriend left him. <u>His life is empty.</u>
3. I was afraid my boss would want me to work this weekend. <u>My heart sank</u> when the phone rang.
4. Your point of view is interesting. But I'm afraid <u>your argument has holes in it</u>!
5. The patient suffered from cancer. After three months, she gave up <u>the battle.</u>
6. My son had an accident in my car. Boy, am I <u>burned up</u>!
7. I was feeling so depressed. But, seeing you always <u>gives me a lift</u>!
8. Can't you find any better ideas? That one is so <u>old hat</u>!
9. I hope George doesn't come to work in our department. He's such a <u>pain in the neck</u>!
10. I doubt that Maria and Rob will stay together. I think their <u>marriage is dead</u>.

WRAP UP

A Synthesis

Each of the three poems in this unit focuses on a particular season: winter, spring, and fall. The poets use certain vocabulary to create the picture of a particular season.

Read the poems on pages 166–167. Make a list of words and expressions that describe the season of each poem. One example from each poem has been given.

Poems	Vocabulary that produces feelings of the season
Winter "Stopping by Woods on a Snowy Evening"	*snowy*
Spring "when faces called flowers float out of the ground"	*flowers*
Fall "Late October"	*October*

B Analysis

Poetry usually has both rhythm and rhyme.

Rhythm is the pattern of stressed and unstressed syllables in a poem. Sometimes rhythm is a defined, repeated pattern in poetry (called *meter*). Other times, rhythm is not a defined pattern. This kind of open-form poetry changes its rhythm, like in some music. Some poems have *visual rhythm*. In other words, the physical length of a poem's lines change. They go in; they go out. They get shorter; they get longer. This adds to the whole feeling of the poem.

Rhyme is the repetition of similar sounds. Many poems have rhyme at the end of lines of poetry. This is especially true of traditional poetry. Sometimes poems repeat the same sounds in other parts of the poem. Many newer forms of poetry have no rhyme.

Rhythm

Match each poem to the description of its rhythm.

"Stopping by Woods on a Snowy Evening"	There is no defined rhythm, but there is visual rhythm.
"when faces called flowers float out of the ground"	Each stanza (group of lines) has a pattern: 11, 12, 12, 11, 12, 12, 10 beats (syllables).
"Late October"	There are 8 beats (syllables) in every line.

Rhyme

Match each poem to the description of its rhyme.

"Stopping by Woods on a
Snowy Evening"

Lines 1, 2, and 4 rhyme; the last
word in the third line becomes the
rhyming word for the next stanza

"when faces called flowers float
out of the ground"

There is no rhyme.

"Late October"

There is no ending rhyme, but sounds
are repeated throughout the poem.

ⓒ Creation

Each poem you have studied in this unit is related to a different season of the
year. Probably the most famous type of poetry that includes a seasonal theme is
haiku, a form of traditional Japanese poetry.

Haiku is a 17-syllable verse form consisting of 5, 7, and 5 syllables. This is a rule
in Japanese, but in English the rule is more flexible. Structure and rhythm are
important in haiku. Rhyme is not important.

Haikus can describe almost anything, but they always give a reader a new
experience with a well-known situation. Each haiku must have a seasonal word
(a *kigo*), which tells us in which season the haiku is set. For example, *cherry
blossoms* indicate spring, *snow* indicates winter, and *mosquitoes* indicate
summer. Here are some classic haiku translated from Japanese into English.
Each one represents a different season.

Spring

Covered with the flowers
Instantly I'd like to die
In this dream of ours!

    —*Etsujin (1656?–1739)*

Fall

First autumn morning:
the mirror I stare into
shows my father's face.

    —*Murakami, Kijo (1865–1938)*

Summer

A giant firefly:
that way, this way, that way, this—
and it passes by.

    —*Issa, Yoshi Mikami (1762–1826)*

Winter

A mountain village
under the piled-up snow
the sound of water.

    —*Shiki, Masaoka (1867–1902)*

*Write your own haiku. Choose a season. Keep the structure simple. Try the 5, 7, 5
syllable verse. (Or you can use a different structure). Be sure to use vocabulary that
will produce a feeling of your season. Read your haiku to the class. You may want
to record all of the students' haiku.*

Information Gap Activities

UNIT 1, LISTENING 2

F Looking at Language

2. *Work in pairs. Student A reads a statement. Student B reads the response with either the –ing or –ed adjective. Student A corrects Student B's answer. Change roles after item 5.*

Student B

1. I was very (interesting/interested). The instructor taught me many new things!

2. It was so (exciting/excited)! Let's do it again.

3. No, I think I would be (boring/bored) skiing for a whole week. Let's just stay the weekend.

4. It's so (depressing/depressed). I haven't been in good enough shape to ski.

5. I don't know. I think this sport is really (tiring/tired). I'm going to bed!

6. How do you feel after skiing down that steep mountain? (Answer: *satisfied*)

7. Look at that snowboarder! He looks beautiful coming down that mountain.(Answer: *amazing*)

8. You skied down that mountain perfectly! (Answer: *surprised*)

9. How did you feel looking at the scenery from the top of the mountain? (Answer: *moved*)

10. Did you like your snowboard instructor today? (Answer: *amusing*)

UNIT 10, LISTENING 2

F Looking at Language

2. *In English, certain verbs are followed by gerunds. Work in pairs. Take turns asking questions about spring. Use the correct gerund form. Your partner will check your questions. Write your partner's answers.*

Student B

1. *(Partner's question: What do you enjoy eating in the spring?)*

2. Is there anything you mind _____ (do) in the spring?

   Answer: _____

3. *(Partner's question: What do you avoid buying in the spring?)*

4. Where do you suggest _____ (go) during spring vacation?

   Answer: _____

5. *(Partner's question: What did you regret doing last spring?)*

6. What will you consider _____ (do) next spring?

   Answer: _____

7. *(Partner's question: Where can you imagine being in the spring?)*

8. What did you quit _____ (do) last spring?

   Answer: _____

9. *(Partner's question: What do you miss doing in the spring?)*

10. What do you like _____ (see) every spring?

    Answer: _____

Audioscript

Unit 1 Selling a Dream

LISTENING 1: NEW YORK STATE LOTTERY AD

B. Listening for the Main Ideas

Come and listen to our story 'bout a girl named Jen
Livin' upstate with her husband named Ben
Then one day when she stopped to get some gas
She picked the winning numbers,
And she won a ton of cash.
(Millions that is . . . lots of zeros!)

Well the next thing you know
Young Jen's a millionaire,
Ben's got new clothes and he's lookin' debonair.
Told the travel agent "Gotta get away soon,"
So they jumped on a plane to their second honeymoon.
(And then a third . . . and a fourth after that!)

Now Ben and Jen are lookin' mighty tan,
Smiling ear to ear, and walkin' hand-in-hand.
Say they can't believe just how pale they used to be 'till they got the winning numbers in the New York Lottery.

New York Lotto. New York's mega-millions! It can happen, ya hear?

Announcer: For New York Lottery, winning results, call 1-900-336-2020. Calls are 40 cents a minute. Call 1-900-336-2020

C. Listening for Details
Repeat Listening for the Main Ideas.

D. Listening for Inference

Now Ben and Jen are lookin' mighty tan,
Smiling ear to ear, and walkin' hand-in-hand.
Say they can't believe just how pale they used to be 'till they got the winning numbers in the New York Lottery.

LISTENING 2: OKEMO SKI RESORT AD

B. Listening for the Main Ideas

Ah, yes. The pure, sweet sound of skis and snowboards carving into the freshly groomed snow at Okemo Mountain in Vermont. Listen! (*people yelling*) That's the sound of people enjoying the best conditions in the East. Little do they know that Okemo snow groomers were up all night, sculpting that snow like the frosting on your Aunt Tilly's icebox cake. Listen! (*sound of snowboarders*)
That's the sound of riders in the Okemo super pipe performing their gravity-defying deeds of daring on snow groomed wall-to-wall.
"Sick pipe, dude."
"If you say so, dude."
So, whatever Mother Nature dishes out, Okemo can take it and make it into conditions that leave you feeling like this: (*people shouting happily*)
So, don't settle for snow that's been neglected and disrespected. Go for snow that's treated like white gold. Go to Okemo! It's always fresh.

C. Listening for Details
Repeat Listening for the Main Ideas.

LISTENING 3: CUPID.COM AD

B. Listening for the Main Ideas

MAN: Somewhere on this radio station, out in the ether, there's someone looking for you.
Woman: Yeah, right.
Man: Don't be so negative. There is someone just for you.
Woman: Me?
Man: Yes, you.
Woman: Really?
Man: Yes.
Woman: Really and truly?
Man: Now you're getting on my nerves. There is someone listening to this same radio station who'd love to meet you. Like the person in the car next to you.
Woman: Oh, he's cute!
Man: As a button. Well, you'll find Mr. Button . . . uh, you'll find him on Cupid.com.
Woman: Cupid.com?
Man: What is it with you repeating things? At Cupid.com you can browse thousands of people in your area who are also looking for someone just like you.
Woman: Me?
Man: Are we going to start this again?
Woman: Sorry.
Man: Cupid.com. Registration is free, and no one knows who you are until you want them to know who you are.

Woman: Sounds too good to be true!

Man: Well, it's true. Now I have 150,000 other men and women to talk to today, so goodbye. And that's a nice skirt you're wearing.

Woman: Thanks. Wait. Do you tell that to everyone?

Man: I skip that part for the men. Bye, and remember:

Chorus: "Don't be stupid. Go to Cupid. Dot com that is."

Man: I hope the next one's a little brighter.

C. Listening for Details

Repeat Listening for the Main Ideas.

D. Listening for Inference

Man: Somewhere on this radio station, out in the ether, there's someone looking for you.

Woman: Yeah, right.

Man: Don't be so negative. There is someone just for you.

Woman: Me?

Man: Yes, you.

Woman: Really?

Man: Yes.

Woman: Really and truly?

WRAP UP

B. Analysis

Repeat Listening 1, Listening 2, Listening 3.

Unit 2 Pet Advice

LISTENING 1: "DOG BARKS WHILE I'M OUT"
WITH JON KATZ

B. Listening for the Main Ideas

Host: Go to Leslie now, in Highland. Hi, Leslie.

Leslie: Hi. How are you?

Host: Doin' fine.

Leslie: Thanks for taking my call.

Host: Sure.

Leslie: Uh, I have a . . . about a five-and-a-half-year-old beagle . . . I've had since he was two. I just recently moved like the beginning of February. I live in an apartment house with four apartments, and when he's left alone, he'll bark. Um . . . I don't know whether he did this where I used to live before . . . I never got any complaints. Um . . . I just wondered if there's anything I could do.

Jon: Is he loose in the house?

Leslie: Yes.

Jon: Yeah. Have you tried putting him in a . . . How long are you leaving him alone? Just a few hours at a stretch?

Leslie: Yeah, actually no more than that. Sometimes an hour, two hours. I mean sometimes it could be four or five hours, but . . .

Jon: Right. Has he ever been crated?

Leslie: Uh, he was crated when he was very young . . . well when we first got him. He was two when we got him, so he was crated then.

Jon: Well, here's what I've . . . what I've done when that problem—and I have 100 percent success rate—is . . . I get a good-sized crate, especially if it's not too many hours, and put a bone in it, and put some water in it, and cover it with a towel or a blanket, you know so that it's mostly covered. Obviously make sure that the ventilation and all is good, and there's water. And just leave him in there. And I bet you money the barking stops.

Leslie: OK, now there's a dog across the hall that barks, and I think that's what starts it. Would that still help if the dog across the hall still barks?

Jon: It would help because, you know, people have this idea that since it would be cruel to put a human in a crate, it's cruel to put a dog in a crate. But in fact what is great for certain dogs, and some dogs don't need it obviously—my dogs need it because when they're in the crate and it's covered, they're off the clock. They don't feel responsible. They go into a nice state of what the trainers call "doggie Zen" . . .

Leslie: OK. (*laughs*)

Jon: . . . where they kind of just relax. It's very good for many dogs. It actually helps them to be calm and says to them, "You know what? You're off the clock now. You're a great dog. You're working very hard. You can just take a couple of hours off."

Leslie: OK.

Jon: If that doesn't work, um, you know there are other things you can try. You can try, you know, desensitization to sound, but that's complicated. You can also try putting them in a different room, or even putting them in a different place. I would try the crate, though.

Leslie: OK, now another thing I had was . . .

Host: No, Leslie, I'm sorry. We are . . . we're out of time. Show's over, but you can call again next time.

Leslie: OK, sorry. (*laughs*)

Jon: Bye-bye.

Host: Leslie, thanks so much for the call.

C. Listening for Details

Repeat Listening for the Main Ideas.

D. Listening for Inference

Jon: Yeah. Have you tried putting him in a . . . How long are you leaving him alone? Just a few hours at a stretch?

Leslie: Yeah, actually no more than that. Sometimes an hour, two hours. I mean sometimes it could be four or five hours, but . . .

LISTENING 2: "Dog Eats Anything"
with Sue Sternberg

B. Listening for the Main Ideas

Host: Let's move on to Jodi in Hurley, who has a pug that eats anything. That's what my note says. (*laughs*)

Jodi: Hi.

Host: Hi, Jodi. You're on the air.

Jodi: Hi. Thank you for taking my call. I have a . . . almost three-year-old pug, and . . . um . . . she eats twice day. We got her when she was six months old, and ever since she's been a puppy, um . . . we try to keep things out of her reach that could be harmful to her, and we thought she'd outgrow it, but she . . . this morning I found her with a big, metal screw in her mouth, chasing her around the house to try and get it out . . .

Sue: OK . . .

Jodi: . . . because I don't want her to end up damaging her intestines . . . that sort of thing.

Sue: Right.

Jodi: So, if you could give me some tips or hints on what to do . . .

Sue: What does she, um . . . is it metal, or is it plastic . . . is it anything?

Jodi: Anything.

Sue: And how often . . . like, what would you say . . . give me on a daily . . . a list of things she might get into.

Jodi: Um . . . anytime if my children were to drop something that . . . you know, she happens to be in the room, if she sees it, she'll bolt towards it and grab it and take off with it. Or, if she's in a room by herself and just happens to discover that there's a piece of plastic or something that she can reach, she'll grab at it, and . . .

Sue: OK.

Jodi: . . . she has balls, and toys and bones, but she's always searching out something else.

Sue: OK. What it may be is . . . she likes the game. And the game is when she has something forbidden, everyone in the family wakes up, looks at her, chases her, and she might think that is a wonderful game, even though you might be angry or worried.

Jodi: Uh-huh.

Sue: And what happens is she picks up her own toy and nothing happens. So, she learns very quickly that things like screws and eyeglasses and remote controls and plastic baggies, and whatever else, all the forbidden items get this wonderful game going, where the whole family gets involved, and all of her toys are, you know, sort of dead in the water.

Jodi: Uh-huh.

Sue: What you want to do . . . I would, um, and make it a whole family thing – get down on your hands and knees and go around the house and puppy-proof as if you've just brought a new puppy home . . . puppy-proof the house, pick up any of these odds and ends, you know pick up anything that might cause a problem. Buy her a series of, um, new and safe toys, and try to match the textures and materials of the items that she likes to feel. Like if she likes metal, they don't make any metal toys, but you might try to get a toy that's hard, very hard, or, you know, um, is most similar to that. If she likes cloth, buy her a cloth toy.

Jodi: OK.

Sue: And what you want to do is a new game with a kid, when she grabs one of the new toys, everyone will get up, they'll call her name, run around the house, you don't have to chase her . . .

Jodi: (*laughs*)

Sue: . . . but have this huge explosive fun game.

Jodi: (*laughs*) OK.

Sue: And pet her and talk to her and throw it and take, you know, just huge thing. If she picks up a forbidden item, everyone, everyone, and I don't care what's on TV or who's watching a video, or who's on the computer, when she picks up . . . let's say she has a screw in her mouth, I want the family entirely . . . have a code word. And everyone stands up and runs into the bathroom and closes the door and leaves her out.

Jodi: (*laughs*) Gosh, so she's isolated, and she knows no one's giving her a reaction.

Sue: Right. And what usually happens is . . . try it once, you get into the bathroom. Everyone counts to 10. You come back out. If she's still chewing the item and doesn't care that you've all run into the bathroom, don't bother doing it, 'cause you'll just have a dog that eats these things, but 99 times out of 100, what happens is you'll come out of the bathroom and the screw— or whatever's been in her mouth—will be on the floor and she'll be at the door wondering why everyone left.

Jodi: (*laughs*) OK.

Sue: OK? So what she'll learn is when she grabs forbidden items, it makes you disappear instantly.

Jodi: And when she's got the toys that . . .

Sue: . . . huge fun . . .

Jodi: . . . you approve of, she gets a big rally.

Sue: Yeah. OK?

Jodi: OK. Well, that'll be helpful. We'll give that a try.

Sue: Good luck. Have fun.

Jodi: OK. Thanks so much. Bye-bye.

Host: Bye-bye. There's a fun game. When you have family and friends over . . .

Sue: Yeah. They'll think you're crazy . . .

Host: . . . let's all go run and hide in another room.

C. Listening for Details

Repeat Listening for the Main Ideas.

D. Listening for Inference

EXCERPT 1:

Sue: OK. What it may be is . . . she likes the game. And the game is when she has something forbidden, everyone in the family wakes up, looks at her, chases her, and she might think that is a wonderful game, even though you might be angry or worried.

Jodi: Uh-huh.

EXCERPT 2:

Sue: And what happens is she picks up her own toy and nothing happens. So, she learns very quickly that things like screws and eyeglasses and remote controls and plastic baggies, and whatever else, all the forbidden items get this wonderful game going, where the whole family gets involved, and all of her toys are, you know, sort of dead in the water.

Jodi: Uh-huh.

EXCERPT 3:

Sue: And what you want to do is a new game with a kid, when she grabs one of the new toys, everyone will get up, they'll call her name, run around the house, you don't have to chase her . . .

Jodi: (*laughs*)

Sue: . . . but have this huge explosive fun game.

Jodi: (*laughs*) OK.

LISTENING 3: "CAT HIERARCHY"
WITH SUE STERNBERG

B. Listening for the Main Ideas

Host: Let's go to Kathleen in Niskayuna right now. This is a cat question for Sue Sternberg. You're on the air. Go ahead please.

Kathleen: Yes, hi. Um, I think I know the answer to what I have to do, but I'm just looking for a little extra guidance.

Sue: OK.

Kathleen: I have three cats who have been introduced to the household at different times, and cat number 1 has been around for about five years, from a shelter; cat number 2, who's still a kitten, joined our house in August of last year . . .

Sue: OK.

Kathleen: . . . and then cat number 3 just came around in January. Uh, he was a stray who needed a house, and so, and the kitten needed a playmate . . . so, it was one of those types of situations.

Sue: Uh-huh.

Kathleen: Well, after about two, three weeks, cat number 1 and 3 don't get along.

Sue: OK.

Kathleen: And . . . so . . . we've separated them, and we're about to move, and so I was thinking I need to go through the re-introduction . . .

Sue: Yeah . . .

Kathleen: . . . process again, but wait until we move.

Sue: That's what I would do. Are they having bloody fights? Are either of them ending up at the vet?

Kathleen: No. I think what's happening is number 3 wants to play, and number 1 says "No way!" And she's the only female of the three, number 1, and she is really just somewhat anti-social and just wants to be left alone.

Sue: OK. Um, then I would do exactly as . . . your own advice. Wait till you move. Separate them completely. Do the thing where you, you know, take a cloth and brush one cat and then use the cloth underneath the food bowl to feed the other cat.

Kathleen: Food bowl, right. And then switch the rooms after awhile, too, and that sort of thing?

Sue: I wouldn't switch the rooms, although if that's worked for you in the past, then go for it! What I would . . . I would keep them in their rooms . . . actually go ahead and switch the rooms. I don't see a problem with that. And I would just . . . um . . . um . . . when, let one of the cats out so that . . . um . . . the room . . . or have the rooms meet so that after they stop growling, and they can be stroked by cloths that smell like the other cat, they can meet through just a crack in the door . . .

Kathleen: OK.

Sue: . . . so that they can, um, not, you know, scratch each other, but they can sniff and work that out. When there's no growling, when there's a crack in the door, and they can see each other . . . then you might move to a gate, you know, a baby gate or a screen or something like that, and then just proceed really slowly.

Kathleen: Is there a particular order? Like should the oldest cat . . . get the first option . . .

Sue: Yes . . .

Kathleen: . . . to roam the house first, those types of things?

Sue: Yes. Uh-huh.

Kathleen: OK.

Sue: I mean hierarchy and status and rank is much less so in cats than dogs, but it's there.

And that would be a good thing. And the other thing is get in the habit of really playing with and tiring out your younger cat with an interactive like chase-pounce toy so that his play behaviors are being satisfied. You know, at least 10 minutes twice a day with a game, with you . . .

Kathleen: OK.

Sue: . . . which will deflect some of stuff that he wants to do with the older cat.

Kathleen: OK, that's good. And one last thing . . . the kitten, he gets along with both of them. And, you know, he's so fun and playful, and I worry about having to separate all three of them because he just likes them both. Is that going to be necessary, or if I let him be the one loose cat while I'm trying to reintroduce the two older ones, is that going to put him higher up on the totem pole, I guess I'm asking?

Sue: My guess is that it'll be OK, and I think what I would do is just put the new male in a room by itself, and leave your old cat and the kitten loose.

Kathleen: OK.

Sue: And then a couple of times a day, let the kitten in with the new cat, and let them play.

Kathleen: OK, alright, that's a great idea. Excellent. Thank you so much.

Host: Thanks, thanks, Kathleen.

Kathleen: OK, bye-bye.

Host: Right. Right.

C. Listening for Details
Repeat Listening for the Main Ideas.

D. Listening for Inference

Kathleen: Food bowl, right. And then switch the rooms after awhile, too, and that sort of thing?

Sue: I wouldn't switch the rooms, although if that's worked for you in the past, then go for it! What I would . . . I would keep them in their rooms . . . actually go ahead and switch the rooms. I don't see a problem with that.

Unit 3 Boyhood Memories

LISTENING 1: "A WONDERFUL LIFE"
BY DAVID GREENBERGER

B. Listening for the Main Ideas

It's been a wonderful life. I enjoyed my boyhood. I don't believe anybody enjoyed their boyhood more than I did. What I was doing was what made it wonderful. Maybe I got it from my grandfathers—on both sides—they were woodworkers, so when I got going I kind of turned in that direction. And I liked to make gadgets, I liked to make things, and I started out around eight years old—well, I started out at three years old I guess, four years old, making a tent in the living room out of quilts.

I'll tell you a few of things when I was growin' up that made my boyhood as nice as it was. I was a boy. I was a real cowboy too. When the yo-yos first came into existence, as far as I can go back, it's around 1927, that's the first ones I saw, and of course I was quite young then. Well, I liked to make things, so what did I do? I was rummaging around in the garbage one day, and I found a thing that you put in rugs, you know, to roll them, like a core, and on the end there they had a flange on it. And I got two of those. And I made me a yo-yo, but it was a big yo-yo, a couple feet around. And of course, the only way you could use it, I figured I'd have to crawl up on top of the house, and that's what I did. I crawled up on the house, and that was pretty dangerous because, when you let that yo-yo down, by the time it goes down to the ground and comes back up, it's movin'! I mean, it's really flyin' and you know there's some weight to it. Well, that's one of the things. That's one of the many things I did when I was a boy.

I made a stagecoach one time. I put a seat up front, you know. The only thing about it was, I couldn't get enough boys to pull it! That thing was as big as that chest of drawers. It had doors on it and the seat up on top. I enjoyed making that. We lived in what they call today a duplex house, and the lady that lived there had an Airedale dog, you know one of those fuzzy and ugly lookin' dogs, just as gentle and nice a dog, though, as you'll ever hope to get, and they had one of those. So we'd come down there on our stagecoach, down the sidewalk, and I'd jump down to open the door and this Airedale dog would jump in there, and we'd close it and go on down the road. Things like that. I didn't have a dog until later. My dad gave me a dog after I was married, 'cause I didn't turn in that direction, I didn't want to be what you see on

television, that was all those animals and all that—no, that didn't interest me at all. I just wanted to make something. I always wanted to make things.

You heard of that song "I Enjoy Being a Girl"?—there's a song about that. Well, I enjoyed bein' a boy, and especially a cowboy, or any kind of a boy. I really enjoyed bein' a boy, and the experiences. I can think and remember in detail even the hinges on that stagecoach, which was made out of leather. I can remember in detail what the leather looked like when I made those hinges and I nailed them on there so the doors opened. Things like that. I can't remember what happened yesterday. If you asked me something I might say, "Well, it has faded out." But I can remember those hinges and that stagecoach and that yo-yo.

C. Listening for Details
Repeat Listening for the Main Ideas.

D. Listening for Inference

EXCERPT 1:
I'll tell, you a few things when I was growin' up that made my boyhood as nice as it was. I was a boy. I was a real cowboy too.

EXCERPT 2:
You heard of that song "I Enjoy Being a Girl"?—there's a song about that. Well, I enjoyed bein' a boy, and especially a cowboy, or any kind of boy. I really enjoyed bein' a boy, and the experiences.

LISTENING 2: "A DEATH IN THE FAMILY" BY MARTIN JACOBSON

B. Listening for the Main Ideas

There was a lot of tragedy early on. I had a brother who died at the age of 13, and I must have been about six. It was the most devastating thing that can happen to a family . . . to lose a child. (And his name was?) Sydney. It threw a pall over the house forever. It was like, how can you be happy? Sydney is . . . Sydney died. (And died of?) Spinal meningitis. I think it hit my parents very hard but in different ways. My father was a very sweet, loving, not bombastic, quiet guy, and I think his emotions were rather fragile. And when he lost his son, he went into what was then called a nervous breakdown. I could see something was wrong. I was only six. He wasn't going to work, and here he was playing games with the kids. And I'd ask my mother, "Why is my father not going to work?" And she gave me some excuse, that he's not feeling well, and I didn't know enough. In my mother's case, she wouldn't let go of me. It sounds ridiculous, but she insisted on dressing me in the morning to go to school. Now I'd be sitting on a kitchen table, and she'd be putting my socks and shoes on, and I'd say, "Ma, let me do this." (And how old were you?) I was probably around 10 . . . 12. I mean you don't do that. You lose a lot of self-confidence from things like that. I guess she was afraid of losing me, but I never remember my mother putting her arms around me. She couldn't kiss me, couldn't put her arms around me. My father would, but she couldn't.

C. Listening for Details
Repeat Listening for the Main Ideas.

D. Listening for Inference

EXCERPT 1:
Now I'd be sitting on a kitchen table, and she'd be putting my socks and shoes on, and I'd say, "Ma, let me do this." (And how old were you?) I was probably around 10, . . . 12. I mean you don't do that.

EXCERPT 2:
I guess she was afraid of losing me, but I never remember my mother putting her arms around me. She couldn't kiss me, couldn't put her arms around me. My father would, but she couldn't.

LISTENING 3: "YOUNG ROMANCE"
BY NOAH ADAMS

B. Listening for the Main Ideas

On this 14th day of February, I guess, yes indeed, three decades ago, we all went muffled up through the snow, wearing black rubber buckle-up-the-front boots, off to the moist, wet, wool heat of a sixth-grade classroom in an old brick building. And that room was the world, when you're 12 years old.

We were excited and nervous on Valentine's Day, taking to school homemade valentines. We had made one for everyone in the class who we liked. And that was the way it worked. In the morning, everybody would put their valentines in a box up on the teacher's desk, and then after

lunch, all the valentines would be passed out. Everyone would start counting. Some kids would get valentines from almost everybody else in the class. Some kids, usually the one or two who always sat way in the back, got no valentines at all. I've often wondered over the years what happened to those kids, the ones in the back. But I never assumed, even then, that they were unloved. That's just the way things were in the 6th grade.

After school was out that day, I was off on a more serious affair of the heart. I wasn't satisfied with the schoolroom exchange of valentines. I had somebody special in mind. And I'd been saving money for about a month to buy the biggest and prettiest card I could find and afford for a classmate named Martha Jane. I walked downtown to the drugstore, managed to buy the card with some youthful confidence, and I went over to the park — she lived nearby — and I sat there on the bench and wrote something on the inside of that card, and I was planning on waiting until dark, then going up to her front porch and slipping the valentine into her mailbox. But it must have been what I wrote. I must have said too much because I lost my nerve and tore it up and threw the card and envelope and my incriminating thoughts down into a storm drain and went on home.

There's not a wonderful ending to this story. Martha Jane never did find out what happened. And I managed to find others to worry about sending valentines to, and most of the time I did, and said what I wanted to say. But I know now that I will regret, always, the valentines that remain unsent.

C. Listening for Details
Repeat Listening for the Main Ideas.

D. Listening for Inference
Repeat Listening for the Main Ideas.

Unit 4 Safety

LISTENING 1: A WARNING FROM THE FEDERAL TRADE COMMISSION
B. Listening for the Main Ideas
Child: Wait a minute . . . I thought you said it was my turn to go online.

Parent: It is your turn. Look, I've already logged onto your favorite website.

Child: Well, what are you looking for?

Parent: I already found it. It's the section here, that talks about protecting your privacy.

Child: Protecting my what?

Parent: Your privacy, honey. Your personal information. You know, things like your name, address and telephone number. Your password and your email address are private too. See, this part of the website says they can't ask you to give information about yourself without your parents' permission. This way, you can check with me before you give a website any information.

Child: I never saw this on my website before.

Parent: That's because there's a new law that protects children under age 13 while they're online.

Child: Wow! So if all these websites like protecting me, you'll just have to give me more time online for surfing, right?

Parent: Hmm . . . well, we'll have to see about that later.

Announcer: For information about protecting your child's privacy online, call the Federal Trade Commission toll-free at 1-877-FTC-HELP. Or visit ftc.gov.

C. Listening for Details
Repeat Listening for the Main Ideas.

D. Listening for Inference

EXCERPT 1:

Child: Well, what are you looking for?

Parent: I already found it. It's the section here, that talks about protecting your privacy.

Child: Protecting my what?

EXCERPT 2:

Child: Wow! So if all these websites like protecting me, you'll just have to give me more time online for surfing, right?

Parent: Hmm . . . well, we'll have to see about that later.

F. Looking at Language

EXERCISE 2

1. She can't get online right now.
2. I can find that website for you.
3. She can give her personal information.

4. Those websites can ask me for personal information.
5. She can't spend more time online than her brother.
6. You can't call the Federal Trade Commission today.

LISTENING 2: A MESSAGE FROM THE DEPARTMENT OF HOMELAND SECURITY

B. Listening for the Main Ideas

Woman: Certain events are beyond your control. And you need to have some sort of plan in place with respect to your family members.

Announcer: This is a message from the U.S. Department of Homeland Security, recorded by Li Sun Yi, New York City Office of Emergency Management. The topic: Planning for emergencies.

Woman: I would say one of the most important things is to have some sort of communication plan in place so at least, for your own peace of mind, you know that you're going to be able to contact your family. Also that you have enough water and food in your home in case you have to stay there for awhile. We just want to have people know that there are things they can do to help themselves, to help their family members, to help their neighbors in the event something happens. And the important thing is to use common sense, to remain calm.

Announcer: Learn to be prepared. At www.ready.gov, or call for a free brochure, 1-800-BEREADY. That's 1-800-237-3239. A public service message brought to you by the Ad Council.

C. Listening for Details
Repeat Listening for the Main Ideas.

D. Listening for Inference

Woman: Certain events are beyond your control. And you need to have some sort of plan in place with respect to your family members.

Announcer: This is a message from the U.S. Department of Homeland Security, recorded by Li Sun Yi, New York City Office of Emergency Management. The topic: Planning for emergencies.

LISTENING 3: AN ANNOUNCEMENT FROM THE NATIONAL INTERAGENCY FIRE CENTER

B. Listening for the Main Ideas

Announcer: Here's a hot topic about our wild lands and living with the natural role of fire.

Woman: Many of us love to leave the stress of everyday life and relax in a beautiful spot in the wild lands. The campfire completes the picture. If this sounds like you, remember: Play it safe with campfires and outdoor cooking. Keep campfires small and clear the surrounding area of flammable material. Never leave your fire unattended, and keep water nearby. Remember: Sparks fly! Even a small breeze can fan the flames. When it's time to go, drown fires with water and stir in some dirt. With a little campfire care, your spot will be there next time too.

Announcer: This hot topic was made possible by the Teresa and H. John Heinz III Foundation. Learn more about the natural role of fire, how to protect your community, and get the latest fire information. Visit the National Interagency Fire Center website at nifc.gov. That's nifc.gov.

C. Listening for Details

Repeat Listening for the Main Ideas.

WRAP UP

A. Synthesis

Repeat Listening 1, Listening 2 and Listening 3.

Unit 5 Love

LISTENING 1: "Before I Die" by David Roth

B. Listening for the Main Ideas

Before I die I want to be
The richest man in history
I want to have a wealth of friends
Abundant love that never ends

Before I die I want to find
A lover who is soft and kind
And one last piece of cherry pie
That's what I want before I die

Before I die I want to choose
Some different roads and avenues
I want to walk each one in peace
And all my obstacles release

Before I die I want to know
I've told you that I love you so
I love you so, I love you so
That's what I want you to know

Before I die I want to be
The richest man in history
And one last piece of cherry pie
That's what I want before I die

C. Listening for Details

Repeat Listening for the Main Ideas.

D. Listening for Inference

Before I die I want to find
A lover who is soft and kind
And one last piece of cherry pie
That's what I want before I die

F. Looking at Language

Exercise 2, Part B

1. shin
2. seen
3. dial
4. dime
5. mill
6. wheel
7. sit
8. tile

LISTENING 2: "My Lost Valentine" by Cosy Sheriden

B. Listening for the Main Ideas

i would have sent you roses
once upon a time
roses with a card that just said "shine"
like you do, like we did, does love
forgive every time
roses, my lost valentine
i would have met you in New York
once upon a time

i would have held your hand
in the longest Broadway line
but the sweeter the bloom, the sharper the vine
roses, my lost valentine
roses

could you have loved me through the winter
once upon a time
in cold February
when the mirror is unkind
when the flowers have all faded,
when love is no longer blind
i would have sent you roses
my lost valentine
roses

i would have sent you roses
but it would not be kind

to whoever it is,
is your this year's valentine
who must someday find the thorn
that you prefer your love blind
roses, my lost valentine
roses
i would have sent you roses
once upon a time
roses with a card that just said "shine"

C. Listening for Details

Repeat Listening for the Main Ideas.

LISTENING 3: "THE FRIENDSHIP WALTZ" BY LUI COLLINS

B. Listening for the Main Ideas

I would welcome your presence back into my life
With an ear to ear grin I would greet you on sight
I would dance until dawn, I would laugh at the rain
I would welcome your friendship again.

I can hear your soft voice on the telephone line
I can see your sweet smile as it flits `cross my mind
I can feel your heart, so full within mine
But I cannot look into your eyes.

Though I well understand our paths drawn apart
I still feel the longing deep in my heart
I must patiently wait till faith, hope, love, the trine
Can allow us together in time.

We have chosen this distance, from a deep place
of knowing,
That each one of us may have space for growing
And the mirror we turn, and the honor we share
Hold a promise to always be there.

And though I well understand our paths drawn
apart,
I still feel the longing so deep in my heart
I will patiently wait till faith, hope, love, the trine
Will invite us together in time.

And then I'll welcome your presence back into
my life
And with an ear to ear grin I shall greet you on
sight
I will dance until dawn, I will laugh at the rain
I will welcome your friendship again
I will welcome your friendship again.

C. Listening for Details

Repeat Listening for the Main Ideas.

Unit 6 Volunteering

LISTENING 1: "DISCOVER THE JOY IN SERVING OTHERS" BY AMBER COFFMAN

B. Listening for the Main Ideas

I was eight years old when I realized what it was that I had to do. I was walking down the street and I saw so many homeless men and women. I knew I had to find a way to help. Two years later, I started a nonprofit group to feed the homeless.

Hi, my name is Amber Coffman and today I'm 20 years old. For the past 10 years, the organization I created, Happy Helpers for the Homeless, has delivered love, food, and clothing directly to men and women living on the streets. We've also helped other young people discover the joy in serving others.

You know there's something you need to do in your community. But maybe you thought, "What can I do? I'm just one person?" You'll be amazed at what a difference you can make, if you just put your mind to it. Decide today to make that difference.

Get out and live—volunteer!

Brought to you by the Hitachi Foundation's Yoshiyama Award for Exemplary Service to the Community and this station.

C. Listening for Details

Repeat Listening for the Main Ideas.

D. Listening for Inference

You know there's something you need to do in your community. But maybe you thought, "What can I do? I'm just one person?"

LISTENING 2: "FIND ONE HOUR A WEEK" BY REGINA GRANT

B. Listening for the Main Ideas

I was lucky growing up. I had a strong family and support system to tell me that I could be somebody, that I could do something important after high school. But, as I got ready to graduate, I thought . . . what about other kids who don't have that kind of support?

Hi, I'm Regina Grant, I'm 19 years old, and a member of the Maha Nation. I decided to start a mentoring program for Native students. We help kids see that a college education is something they can achieve and be successful in. We also teach them about their Native heritage and where they come from.

The young people who volunteer to be mentors in our program commit just one hour a week of their time. It's not much time, but it really makes a difference. Couldn't you find one hour a week to volunteer in something you believe in? So many people in every community need our help.

Get out and live—volunteer!

C. Listening for Details
Repeat Listening for the Main Ideas.

D. Listening for Inference
Repeat Listening for the Main Ideas.

LISTENING 3: "A NEED TO FILL" BY WREX PHIPPS

B. Listening for the Main Ideas

Growing up on a farm out here, I just thought life was great. I had my own horse. I drove a tractor with my dad. For me, I thought farm life was the American Dream. Hi, my name is Wrex Phipps.

That all changed when I was reminded how dangerous working on a farm can be. My cousin was almost killed in a terrible accident. I had to do something. I couldn't help my cousin. But I could help other people avoid this on their farms.

So I volunteered at farm safety day camps for children of all ages, teaching kids about being safe around tractors, tools, and animals.

Just like I found a need to fill in my community, your community needs you. Find out how you can help in your hometown.

Get out and live—volunteer!

C. Listening for Details
Repeat Listening for the Main Ideas.

D. Listening for Inference

Growing up on a farm out here, I just thought life was great. I had my own horse.
I drove a tractor with my dad. For me, I thought farm life was the American Dream.

Unit 7 Life Lessons

LISTENING 1: "THE DOVE AND THE ANT" BY DIANE MACKLIN

B. Listening for the Main Ideas

There was a dove who was perched on a branch, enjoying the wonderful summer day when she heard a little tiny voice calling out, "Help me. Help me." She looked down and there was an ant in the river. She flew down and rescued that ant and put him on the shore. "Ant, friend, the river is no place for you. You could have drowned." And that ant said, "Oh, thank you, dove. I so appreciate that you saved me, and, you know, one day, I'll help you. Yes, one day I'll help you."

Now the dove, she looked at ant, "Oh, (dove) thank you for the offer, but you're too tiny to help someone like me, but once again, thank you. Thank you for offering." And she flew back into the tree. But the ant knew that she could help. And there was a hunter that came along, and the dove was just admiring the sky and enjoying the day so much that she did not notice that hunter. But the ant did. And, when that ant saw that hunter, she crawled over to him, climbed up his pants leg, and bit him. "Ow!" That hunter howled in the air. The dove looked and saw that the hunter almost was ready to shoot her. She flew away, and the ant crawled down his pants and walked away. Later on that day, the dove came over and found that ant and she said, "Oh, thank you, ant. Thank you." And the ant said, "It was no trouble at all."

And that's the dove and the ant.

C. Listening for Details
Repeat Listening for the Main Ideas.

D. Listening for Inference
Repeat Listening for the Main Ideas.

LISTENING 2: "THE PRINCE WHO THOUGHT HE WAS A ROOSTER" BY RENEE BRACHFELD AND MARK NOVAK

B. Listening for the Main Ideas

Once there was a prince who thought he was a rooster. Now, while other princes spent their time learning how to rule the kingdom or courting princesses, or slaying dragons, this prince shed his royal robes, and he spent his days crouched underneath a table, refusing to eat anything except for kernels of corn. His father, the king, was rather upset by this. He said, "Send for the finest doctors in the land. I'll give a huge reward to anyone who will cure my son." Each of them tried, but none could cure the prince. He still thought that he was a rooster. And he spent his days, crouched underneath that table, refusing to eat anything except for kernels of corn, preening his feathers and crying, "Cock-a-doodle-doo!"

Finally, one day, a wise man was passing through the kingdom. And he came to the king and said, "Give me one week all alone with your son, and I will cure him." The king didn't believe him. He said, "Everybody else has tried and failed, but if you can really do what you say, I'll give you just one week all alone with him." And so, the wise man was shown into the room where the prince stayed. And then, he too shed his robes. He crouched beneath the table near the prince, and he began to eat kernels of corn. The prince was suspicious. "Who are you?" The wise man remained calm. "I am a rooster." And then he went back to munching on the kernels of corn. After a little while, he turned back to the prince and said, "And, um, who are you?" "I, too, am a rooster." And with that, the two of them became good friends. And they spent their days crouched beneath the table, refusing all food except for kernels of corn, preening their feathers and crying, "Cock-a-doodle-doo! Cock-a-doodle-doo!"

Well, after a few days had passed in this manner, the wise man crawled out from under the table, put his fancy robes back on, and then crouched under the table again. The prince was very upset. "Roosters don't wear clothes like that!" "I'm a rooster," insisted the wise man calmly. "And I can dress like this if I want to." Well, the prince thought about this for awhile. And after a short time, he decided to imitate his friend. And he, too, wore clothes. After another day or so had passed, the wise man crawled out from under the table. He went to the door and brought in one of the trays of good food, which had been left for them each day, but which

previously they had both refused to eat. He brought the tray of good food into the room, crouched under the table with it, and began to eat that delicious food. The prince was disgusted. "Roosters don't eat that kind of food!" "You can be a perfectly good rooster," the wise man insisted, "and eat any kind of food you want to." "Hm." Well, the prince thought about that as well. And after a short time, he decided to imitate his friend. And he, too, ate that food.

After another day or so had passed, the wise man crawled out from under the table. He began to walk around the room, standing upright, straight and tall, like a man. The prince was beside himself. "Roosters just don't get up and walk around like that!" "I'm a rooster, and I can walk like this if I choose to," insisted the wise man. The prince thought about this, too, and after a short time decided to imitate his friend. And he, too, walked. And so it was. By the end of the week, the prince no longer acted like a rooster. He wore clothes and ate food and walked like a man.

Well, the king was overjoyed. He welcomed his son back with open arms. Well, as for the wise man, he collected a large reward and happily went on his way.

C. Listening for Details
Repeat Listening for the Main Ideas.

D. Listening for Inference
Repeat Listening for the Main Ideas.

LISTENING 3: "THE LADY IN THE POT" BY MARC SPIEGEL

B. Listening for the Main Ideas

Once there was a lady who lived in a pot. It was made of painted china. She was made of painted china. And had once adorned a beautiful music box with a large fluffy powder puff in a place to hold powder right underneath where she sat. But that was long ago.

Now she lived in a small clay pot that hung on a nail in a forgotten corner of the basement. Now when she'd been a music box, she had always dreamed that a handsome prince would come and waltz with her, and together they would go dancing off into the magic world outside. Those dreams were gone now. The music box smashed the floor long ago, and she was all alone.

One day, the door to the basement opened with the heavy step she had heard so many times before. And suddenly, a small metal frog with green hands and green feet was placed not two inches from her, his legs straddling the rim of the pot. He was covered with white rhinestones or holes where rhinestones had been. His eye was a red jewel. He had been a pin, but his clasp was broken. Close to his heart he held a large mother-of-pearl banjo, and when his hand moved across it, music played. The frog said, "Tell me beautiful maid, what are your dreams? And I will play them for you." But the lady answered, "Go away, frog. When I was young, to laugh and dance was all that mattered. But now, but now I am covered with dust. And all I remember are the thoughts of forgotten dreams and lost hopes. Go play your music someplace else, frog. I have no dreams anymore."

But the frog could go nowhere. So he played anyway. And the lady could go nowhere. So she listened. And the music carried her away from herself . . . as if she had floated up above the pot and all the dust was washed away. And she turned, and there stood the frog with every jewel brightly shining. And they took each other by the hand, and they danced, and they danced, and they danced.

So, remember: Never, never, never, never, never give up your dreams, for they may come to pass when you least expect them.

C. Listening for Details
Repeat Listening for the Main Ideas.

D. Listening for Inference
Repeat Listening for the Main Ideas.

Unit 8 Cooking Tips

LISTENING 1: PREPARING A TURKEY WITH CHEF LARRY

B. Listening for the Main Ideas

Chef Larry: When selecting a turkey, now this is debatable, but I like to give this information out . . . because you can kind of determine where

you want to go with this. When selecting the size of a turkey . . .

Eric: Uh-huh.

Chef Larry: . . . you have to figure at least a pound per person. Sounds like a lot, but you're talking about a bone-in turkey, where the turkey itself represents about 30 percent of the weight of the turkey. So, always consider at least a pound per person, comfortably feeding everyone but also making enough for leftovers.

Eric: Exactly . . . turkey sandwiches.

Chef Larry: Also too consider the convenience of fresh versus frozen. You know, if you're going to be able to run around a couple of days before, like Eric said, pre-order it, make all those arrangements, you have to plan it a little bit when you cook. Um, or frozen, if you're able to get it on a deal. A lot of times now if you buy so many groceries or a certain amount of groceries, they'll give you a free turkey, and it might be frozen. So, you might just want to cook that one up. Make sure that you, you know, you thaw it under refrigeration, which leads me to my other tips about thawing. Always thaw under refrigeration. So, you've got to consider that the turkey itself is going to have to sit under refrigeration for five to seven days to defrost. Very, very important. So, if you have a frozen turkey, make sure you thaw it under refrigeration. When you do have your turkey ready to go, when you're ready to season it and put it in the oven or into the deep fryer, you have to rinse it thoroughly and pat it dry. So, cold water, lots of cold water, pat it dry with paper towels. Now here's some roasting times. These are some great hints because sometimes you ask yourself, you know, how long to roast, you know, how long to let the juices settle, and so on and so forth. So, for a 10 to 12 pound turkey, you want to go to about 2 1/2 to 3 hours. This is 10 to 12 pound turkey. A 12 to 14 pound turkey, you increase that to 2 3/4 hours to 3 1/2 hours.

Eric: At what temperature?

Chef Larry: At about 375, Eric. Yeah, for this. 4 to 16 pounds, excuse me, 14 to 16 pounds, 3 3/4 hours. Sixteen to 18 pounds, 3 1/2 to 4 1/4 hours, 18 to 20 pounds really gets you into that time that you need to prepare a lot ahead of time, 3 3/4 hours to 4 1/2 hours. If you have a turkey that is over 20 hours, excuse me, 20 pounds, you almost have to cook it 20 hours, you have to cook it 4 1/2 hours.

Jamie: God!

Chef Larry: Anyway, we'll post this information and get all this information again at our website here.

Eric: It's really a long cooking day . . . it's one of those days, you know, when you go and . . .

Chef Larry: It is! You gotta start early.

Eric: Yeah.

Jamie: Or even a day before, a couple of days before.

Eric: But the thing is . . . you could even pre-cook it, but of course if you pre-cook it, you need nearly the same time to reheat it.

Chef Larry: Right. Absolutely right.

Eric: It's just one of those things that . . . then it gets dry.

C. Listening for Details

Repeat Listening for the Main Ideas.

D. Listening for Inference

Chef Larry: You have to figure at least a pound per person. Sounds like a lot, but you're talking about a bone-in turkey, where the turkey itself represents about 30 percent of the weight of the turkey. So always consider at least a pound per person, comfortably feeding everyone but also making enough for leftovers.

LISTENING 2: MAKING A PIECRUST WITH RUSS PARSONS

B. Listening for the Main Ideas

Chef Jim Coleman: Well, give us some tips for that because it's obviously fall here, and we've got some beautiful apples coming. Can you give us some quick tips on making some . . .

Russ Parsons: Yeah, some quick tips on baking. I think that most, the thing that most people have the most trouble with in baking is making a piecrust, which is, you know, like one of the most fundamental things. Um . . . and I think that what's important to remember is that the critical thing of . . . there are two critical things about piecrust. One of them you can control, and the other one you can't. Uh, the one that you can control is how the butter is cut or the fat is cut into the flour

determines what the crust is going to be like. Um, if you cut the flour, if you cut the fat into the flour thoroughly, so that you get it to that point where it looks kind of like slightly moistened cornmeal . . .

Chef Jim Coleman: Uh-huh.

Russ Parsons: What you're going to get is a European-style pastry crust. . . . Like a tart crust. Uh, it'll be very short. Uh, which is not a . . . that's a perfectly valid type of crust. It's just a short crust. If you want to have a flaky crust, which is, you know, the kind of the American epitome, what you have to do is, you have to show some restraint. You need to stop cutting the fat into the flour when there are still chunks of butter that are unincorporated . . . or chunks of fat, you know, if you're using Crisco or whatever . . . because what happens is that that fat melts, and the moisture in the fat turns to steam. And that's what provides the air spaces that make a crust seem flaky, rather than short. The only way to make good piecrust is to make piecrust over and over and over again.

Chef Jim Coleman: (*laughs*)

Russ Parsons: It really does come down to a matter of touch and practice. And all of the science in the world isn't going to help you. In fact, you know, the thing that, I took an entire summer and made piecrusts. I made piecrusts everyday because I was a lousy piecrust maker. I'm not a great piecrust maker now. But, what I found . . . the thing that made the biggest difference for me in the quality of my piecrust, once I got the cutting of the fat and the ratio of the ingredients right . . . the thing that made the biggest difference for me was how I held my elbows when I was rolling it out. And that's the kind of level of attention that you have to pay, you know, . . . that's how you develop a touch. You have to remember when you're rolling a piecrust out, you're not smashing it down. You're stretching it. And, so, you know, hold your elbows kind of in a little bit more rather than pressing down on it the way, you know, as a big old macho guy, you know, it's like "I'm gonna beat this piecrust into submission." That never happens. The piecrust always wins.

C. Listening for Details

Repeat Listening for the Main Ideas.

D. Listening for Inference

EXCERPT 1:

Russ Parsons: Um, if you cut the flour, if you cut the fat into the flour thoroughly, so that you get it to that point where it looks kind of like slightly moistened cornmeal. What you're going to get is a European-style pastry crust . . . like a tart crust. Uh, itll be very short. Uh, which is not a . . . that's a perfectly valid type of crust.

EXCERPT 2:

Russ Parsons: And so, you know, hold your elbows kind of in a little bit more rather than pressing down on it the way, you know, as a big old macho guy, you know, it's like "I'm gonna beat this piecrust into submission." That never happens. The piecrust always wins.

LISTENING 3: COOKING STEAK ON A BARBECUE WITH HUGH CARPENTER

B. Listening for the Main Ideas

Hugh Carpenter: Uh, can I just give you a cooking tip?

Interviewer: Great!

Hugh Carpenter: Since we're right in the heart of barbecue season . . .

Interviewer: Yes.

Hugh Carpenter: . . . to tell you the best way to cook any steak that you put on a barbecue . . .

Interviewer: OK.

Hugh Carpenter: . . . that's half an inch or more thick?

Interviewer: Uh-huh.

Hugh Carpenter: I don't care whether you have a gas or a charcoal barbecue. The only way of cooking a steak, or any thicker piece of meat, is to sear it on both sides so it picks up the pattern of the grill on your barbecue. That's about a medium heat. It takes about two minutes to do it on each side. And then to take the steak and to move it away from the heat, on a gas barbecue, that means turning off all the gas jets except one and leaving that one gas jet on the lowest possible setting.

Interviewer: Oh . . .

Hugh Carpenter: And close the barbecue lid, and cook it in an environment that hovers right around 300 degrees. And what will happen is that those rib-eye steaks have been sealed on the outside. They have this nice char from the initial browning, the fat's been rendered out, the barbecue sauce is reduced and caramelized, and it's become more intense in flavor, but now, from now on, you're cooking it indirectly over very, very low heat, and what happens is that you cook the steak, whether it's a one-inch rib-eye steak or a two-inch individual fillet mignon or chateaubriand piece of meat, it cooks it absolutely evenly from edge to edge, whether you want it rare from edge to edge or medium rare from edge to edge. It cooks it totally evenly, and there's no moisture lost in the meat because it's in a much more gentle environment.

Interviewer: Now I would think you would need to practice that a couple of times to get the cooking time down, to get the doneness that you want . . . to figure out for your grill, OK, to get rare or medium rare, once I move it away from the direct heat, I need to do this for how long?

Hugh Carpenter: Right, it's gonna take a little bit longer. . .you know, and you're gonna have a built-in thermometer on your barbecue lid. It's gonna tell you what that environment . . .

Interviewer: Mine never works!

Hugh Carpenter: Well, it should if you have a good thermometer, and you replace that thermometer that your barbecue comes with. And I want to keep it in a 300-degree environment, and on a gas barbecue, if I can't keep it at 300 degrees, even with one burner, just one burner, on low, then I crack the lid open a little bit . . .

Interviewer: Uh-huh.

Hugh Carpenter: So I'm flushing out a little bit of that hot air.

Interviewer: Uh-huh.

Hugh Carpenter: But the whole idea in barbecuing, really is, with a very few exceptions, is a quick sear on both sides, and then cooking the food, and as low an environment, as cool an environment as possible.

Interviewer: Seal in the juices.

Hugh Carpenter: Yeah, and what happens then is you get this incredibly even cooking all the way through without any drying out of the meat.

C. Listening for Details

Repeat Listening for the Main Ideas.

D. Listening for Inference

EXCERPT 1:

Hugh Carpenter: I don't care whether you have a gas or charcoal barbecue. The only way of cooking a steak, or any other thicker piece of meat, is to sear it on both sides so it picks up the pattern of the grill on your barbecue. That's about medium heat. It takes about two minutes to do it on each side. And then to take the steak and to move it away from the heat on a gas barbecue, that means turning off all the gas jets except one and leaving that one gas jet on the lowest possible setting.

Interviewer: Oh . . .

EXCERPT 2:

Interviewer: Now I would think you would need to practice that a couple of times to get the cooking time down, to get the doneness that you want . . . to figure out for your grill, OK, to get rare or medium rare, once I move it away from the direct heat, I need to do this for how long?

Hugh Carpenter: Right, it's gonna take a little bit longer . . . you know, and you're gonna have a built-in thermometer on your barbecue lid. It's gonna tell you what that environment . . .

Interviewer: Mine never works!

WRAP UP

A. Synthesis

Repeat Listening 1, Listening 2, Listening 3.

Unit 9 Women and War

LISTENING 1: JEANNE MARKLE

B. Listening for the Main Ideas

They were 12-hour shifts a day and six days a week. And sometimes you even worked on your day off if the census was very high. And the helicopters after we opened came in all the time everyday. It was a busy hospital. We got a lot of injured.

That was a very emotional time for me. I had just left Brian in Vietnam, and he wasn't going to be coming home for the birth of our baby. And there I am in this belly of this airplane with more than 100 injured soldiers, and that's what I did over there. I took care of those boys, and I couldn't get away from it. It was there all the way home. And so I was pretty depressed on the trip home.

Right across from me there was a blond-headed young man—couldn't have been more than 20—and he had lost both arms, and he was also blind. And he just laid there quietly the whole trip, but at mealtime, of course, the Air Force nurse came with the tray and knelt down beside him and fed him, and it was very emotional for me to watch him. I kept thinking, "Oh this poor, poor boy. How is he going to get through life like this?" I thought, "Gee, if he wasn't blind he'd see the spoon coming, or maybe if he is blind and had his hand, he could feed himself, but this boy was blind with no hands, and he didn't know where the spoon was coming from. And I watched her try to touch his cheek with the spoon so he could turn that way like a new baby to learn to eat again. It was very, very sad.

Coming home wasn't a happy experience at all. Not only did I have my own difficulties to face, I had a nation to face that didn't want to even know about me. And they told me not to wear my uniform home just to pack it up in my suitcase and wear civilian clothes home. I faced people all along the way of my homecoming that didn't want to even know where I came from or what I'd been doing. And I could tell that right away. And we had lived through news bulletins and all the demonstrations. We knew that we weren't appreciated at all. And so it was a very different homecoming than some of your Second World War veterans had gotten. I didn't talk about it. And I even came home to Indiana to a small farming community of 400 people in northern Indiana, and they were glad to say "hi" to me, but they didn't ask me anything, and so it all bottled up inside of me for many, many years.

C. Listening for Details
Repeat Listening for the Main Ideas.

D. Listening for Inference
Repeat Listening for the Main Ideas.

LISTENING 2: MARION GURFEIN

B. Listening for the Main Ideas

After three years they were actually going to let him come home for four weeks. Can you believe what it was like in 1945? You know, how the girls now are going crazy because their husbands are gone a few months? Well, I waited almost three years for Joe. And then to have thirty days with him. So, we were all up in the living room sitting there. Joe's parents, my mother, my sisters. And I heard the elevator come up. Look at me, I'm still trembling. And I ran out into the hall and ran over to the elevator and the door opened and there was Joe, and I guess that was one of the greatest moments of my life. I mean, we fell into each other's arms. And I can't remember exactly what we said, but took him back and presented him with this beautiful little girl.

I was living in a world with all women. And we used to sit in the park. And every now and then a telegram would arrive. And it was either missing-in-action, or dead, and you didn't know what to say to your friends when this happened. So, if it was missing-in-action, you'd say to them, "Oh well, maybe after the war. He's someplace and he can't get in touch with you. But maybe someday you're going to find him again." And, uh, it was a pretty scary, scary time.

C. Listening for Details

Repeat Listening for the Main Ideas.

D. Listening for Inference

EXCERPT 1:

After three years they were actually going to let him come home for four weeks. Can you believe what it was like in 1945? You know, how the girls now are going crazy because their husbands are gone for a few months? Well, I waited almost three years for Joe. And then to have 30 days with him. So, we were all up in the living room sitting there. Joe's parents, my mother, my sisters. And I heard the elevator come up. Look at me, I'm still trembling. And I ran out into the hall and ran over to the elevator and the door opened and there was Joe, and I guess that was one of the greatest moments of my life. I mean, we fell into each other's arms. And I can't remember exactly what we said, but took him back and presented him with this beautiful little girl.

EXCERPT 2:

I was living in a world with all women. And we used to sit in the park. And every now and then a telegram would arrive. And it was either missing-in-action, or dead, and you didn't know what to say to your friends when this happened. So, if it was missing-in-action, you'd say to them, "Oh well, maybe after the war. He's someplace and he can't get in touch with you. But maybe someday you're going to find him again." And, uh, it was a pretty scary, scary time.

LISTENING 3: TOMIKA PERDOMO

B. Listening for the Main Ideas

As a mom, I needed to hear their voices. I needed to know that everything at home was OK. So, it wasn't a distraction for me. Now, some of my male counterparts felt that it was a little bit of a distraction. I think that's when the gender thing comes in. We handle things a little differently. The men knew that their wives at home were taking care of things. They weren't worried about it. Me, on the other hand, I was really concerned. So, I needed to call home or email and hear something back from them to let me know that they're OK. That way I could focus on what I had to do for the Marine Corps.

Because as a single parent, they gave me the option to either go or not to go. If I went, of course I had to have someone watch him. If I did not go, I had to face the choice of being processed out of the Marine Corps. Very hard decision for me at the time, so I called my mother so she could help me out a little bit. And her words were basically, "Did you sign the paper? Did you sign the contract, Tomika?" I said, "Yes, ma'am," and she said, "Well, you know what you have to do then."

He was so big. And I looked at him, I'm thinking, "Wow, Maxine, what have you been feeding my son?" . . . you know? He was so big, and he looked so good. I wanted to hold him, but I didn't want to just push myself on him because he was so young, and he probably didn't really remember who I was anyway. Even though four months to me is a short time, but for a baby, I'm sure it was a pretty long time to not be with your mom. So, I reached out for him, he was in her arms, and he kind of looked at me like, "God, I think I know this lady," but he didn't come to me immediately. He held onto Maxine. And I understood. I really did.

(*gets emotional*) Wow! Whew! And um . . . it really kind of hurt . . . but um . . . but I understood. I let her hold him, and I just looked at him and I told him that I love him . . . and that's pretty much how it was coming home . . . really happy but kind of bittersweet because, you know, you want your baby to know you and to reach out for you. And it kind of didn't happen that way, but I understood.

C. Listening for Details
Repeat Listening for the Main Ideas.

D. Listening for Inference

EXCERPT 1:
As a mom, I needed to hear their voices. I needed to know that everything at home was ok. So, it wasn't a distraction for me. Now some of my male counterparts felt that it was a little bit of a distraction. I think that's when the gender thing comes in. We handle things a little bit differently. The men knew that their wives at home were taking care of things. They weren't worried about it. Me, on the other hand, I was really concerned, so I needed to call home or email and hear something back from them to let me know they're OK. That way I could focus on what I had to do for the Marine Corps.

EXCERPT 2:
Because as a single parent, they gave me the option to either go or not to go. If I went, of course I had to have someone watch him if I did not go, I had to face the choice of being processed out of the Marine Corps. Very hard decision for me at the time so I called my mother so she could help me out a little bit. And her words were basically, "Did you sign the paper? Did you sign the contract, Tomika?" I said, "Yes, ma'am," and she said, "Well, you know what you have to do then."

EXCERPT 3:
So I reached out for him, he was in her arms, and he kind of looked at me like "God, I think I know this lady," but he didn't come to me immediately. He held onto Maxine. And I understood. I really did. (*gets emotional*) Wow! Whew! And um . . . it really kind of hurt . . . but um . . . but I understood. I let her hold him, and I just looked at him and I told him that I loved him . . . and that's pretty much how it was coming

home . . . really happy but kind of bittersweet because you know, you want your baby to know you and to reach out for you. And it kind of didn't happen that way, but I understood.

Unit 10 Seasons
LISTENING 1: "STOPPING BY WOODS ON A SNOWY EVENING" BY ROBERT FROST

B. Listening for the Main Ideas

"Stopping by Woods on a Snowy Evening"
Whose woods these are I think I know.
His house is in the village, though;
He will not see me stopping here
To watch his woods fill up with snow.

My little horse must think it queer
To stop without a farmhouse near
Between the woods and frozen lake
The darkest evening of the year.
He gives his harness bells a shake
To ask if there is some mistake.
The only other sound's the sweep
Of easy wind and downy flake.

The woods are lovely, dark, and deep,
But I have promises to keep,
And miles to go before I sleep,
And miles to go before I sleep.

C. Listening for Details
Repeat Listening for the Main Ideas.

LISTENING 2: "WHEN FACES CALLED FLOWERS FLOAT OUT OF THE GROUND . . ." BY E.E. CUMMINGS

B. Listening for the Main Ideas

when faces called flowers float out of the ground
and breathing is wishing and wishing is having-
but keeping is downward and doubting and never
-it's april(yes,april;my darling)it's spring!
yes the pretty birds frolic as spry as can fly
yes the little fish gambol as glad as can be
(yes the mountains are dancing together)

when every leaf opens without any sound
and wishing is having and having is giving-
but keeping is doting and nothing and nonsense
-alive;we're alive,dear:it's(kiss me now)spring!
now the pretty birds hover so she and so he

now the little fish quiver so you and so i
now the mountains are dancing, the mountains)

when more than was lost has been found has been
    found
and having is giving and giving is living-
but keeping is darkness and winter and cringing
-it's spring(all our night becomes day)o,it's spring!
all the pretty birds dive to the heart of the sky
all the little fish climb through the mind of the sea
all the mountains are dancing;are dancing)

C. Listening for Details

Repeat Listening for the Main Ideas.

LISTENING 3 "LATE OCTOBER"
BY MAYA ANGELOU

B. Listening for the Main Ideas

"Late October"
Carefully
the leaves of autumn

sprinkle down the tinny
sound of little dyings
and skies sated of ruddy sunsets
and roseate dawns
roil ceaselessly in
cobweb greys and turn
to black
for comfort.

Only lovers
see the fall
a signal end to endings
a gruffish gesture alerting
those who will not be alarmed
that we begin to stop
in order simply
to begin
again.

C. Listening for Details

Repeat Listening for the Main Ideas.

Text and Photo Credits

Text: Page 3, **"Couple with All State Results,"** radio advertisement printed with the permission of The New York Lottery, DDB Worldwide Communications Group Inc.; page 7, **"Okemo Mountain Resort,"** radio advertisement printed with the permission of Chris Doyle; page 10, **"You There,"** radio spot printed with the permission of John Tierney, Docsi Corporation, Cupid.com; page 18, **"Dog Barks While I'm Out with Jon Katz,"** segment from pet advice show printed with the permission of Joe Donahue, WAMU (Northeast Public Radio); page 23, **"Dog Eats Anything with Susan Sternberg,"** segment from pet advice show printed with the permission of Joe Donahue, WAMU (Northeast Public Radio); page 27, **"Cat Hierarchy with Susan Sternberg,"** segment from pet advice show printed with the permission of Joe Donahue, WAMU (Northeast Public Radio); page 34, **"Wonderful Life,"** monologue printed with the permission of David Greenberger from his CD, *Mayor of the Tennessee River;* page 38, **"A Death in the Family,"** except from an oral history printed with the permission of Martin Jacobs, StoryCorps.; page 42, **"Young Romance,"** audio segment printed with the permission of Noah Adams; page 61, **"Before I Die,"** 1991 David Roth/ MaytheLight Music (ASCAP), www.davidrothmusic.com, from his CD "Pearl Diver" on Stockfish Records, www.stockfish-records.de~used by permission, David Roth vocal, guitar ocarina, Chris Jones—guitar, Hrolfur Vagnsson—accordion, Hans-Jorg Maucksch—fretless bass; page 64, **"My Lost Valentine,"** love song printed with the permission of Cosy Sheridan from his CD, *Grand Design;* page 68, **"The Friendship Waltz."** Song printed with the permission of Lui Collins; page 75, **"Discover the Joy in Serving Others,"** 2002 Yoshiyama Award Radio Public Service Announcement printed with the permission of Amber Coffman, Jeffrey Rosenberg, Rosenberg Communications, Inc.; page 79, **"Find One Hour a Week,"** 2002 Yoshiyama Award Radio Public Service Announcement printed with the permission of Regina Grant, Jeffrey Rosenberg, Rosenberg Communications, Inc.; page 82, **"A Need to Fill,"** 2002 Yoshiyama Award Radio Public Service Announcement printed with the permission of Wrex Phipps, Jeffrey Rosenberg, Rosenberg Communications, Inc.; page 88, **"The Dove and the Ant,"** excerpt from Kojo Nnamdi Show, printed with the permission of reader, Diane Macklin, WAMU; page 91, **"The Prince Who Thought He Was a Rooster,"** excerpt from the Kojo Nnamdi Show, printed with the permission of readers, Renee Brachfeld and Mark Novak, WAMU; page 95, **"The Lady in the Pot,"** excerpt from the Kojo Nnamdi Show printed with the permission of reader, Mark Spiegel, WAMU; page 103, **"Turkey Tips,"** interview printed with the permission of Ed Keyes, The Chef Larry Show, World Talk Radio; page 107, **"Making a Piecrust with Russ Parsons"** excerpt from **"A Chef's Table,"** interview printed with the permission on Maiken Scott; page 111, **"Cooking Steak on a Barbeque with Hugh Carpenter,"** interview printed with the permission of Ed Keyes, World Talk Radio; page 119, **"Coming Home,"** oral history printed with the permission of Jeanne Markle, Veterans History Project; page 123, **"Coming Home,"** oral history printed with the permission of Marion Gurfein, Veterans History Project; page 126, **"Coming Home,"** interview printed with the permission of Tomika Perdomo, Veterans History Project; page 135, **"Stopping by Woods on a Snowy Evening,"** from the poetry of Robert Frost, edited by Edward Connery Lathe, © 1923, © 1969 by Henry Holt and Company, © 1951 by Robert Frost, reprinted by per mission on Henry Holt and Compant, LLC; page 139, **"when faces called flowers float out of the ground,"** © 1950, © 1978, © 1991 by the Trustees for the ee cummings Trust, © 1979 by George James Firmage, from *E.E. Cummings: Complete Poems 1904-1962* by ee cummings, edited by George J. Firmage, used by permission of Liveright Publishing Corporation; page 142, **"Late October,"** © 1971 Maya Angelou, from *Just Give Me a Cool Drink of Water 'Fore I Die* by Maya Angelou, used by permission of Random House, Inc.

Photos: page 1, © Len Rubenstein/ Index Stock Imagery; page 2, © New York Lottery; page 5, © Jeff Curtes/Corbis; page 9, © Cupid.com; page 16, top; © Ed Bock/Corbis; page 16, bottom left; © Dana Tynan/Corbis; page 16, bottom right; © Trinette Reed/Corbis; page 17, © Paula Span/Brian McLendon; page 21, © Sue Sternberg; page 26, © JA Giordano/Corbis SABA; page 32, © Bettmann/Corbis; page 33, © NMPFT/Kodak Collection/SSPL/The Image Works; page 37, © Bettmann/Corbis; page 40, © Bettmann/Corbis; page 45, top; © Adrian Wyld/Associated Press; page 45, bottom; © Mark Wilson/2003 Getty Images; page 46, © Corbis; page 49, © David Young-Wolff/PhotoEdit; page 54, © Bob Zellar/Associated Press; page 59, top; © Dex Images/Corbis; page 59, middle; © Corbis; page 59, bottom; © Constantinos Loumakis/Corbis; page 60, © Tom Collicott Photography; page 63, © Cosy Sheridan and Mel Strait; page 67, © Susan Wilson/www.susanwilsonphoto.com; page 73, top; © Jeffrey Rosenberg/The Hitachi Foundation:Yoshiyama Awards; page 73, middle; © Jeffrey Rosenberg/The Hitachi Foundation: Yoshiyama Awards; page 73, bottom; © Jeffrey Rosenberg/ The Hitachi Foundation:Yoshiyama Awards; page 74, © Andrew Holbrooke/The Image Works; page 78, © Dartmouth College; page 81, © Corbis; page 86, © Bettmann/Corbis; page 87, © Jim Guzel/www.dianemacklin.com; page 90, © Renee Brachfeld and Mark Novak; page 94, © Marc Spiegel; page 101, left; © Corbis; page 101, middle; © Jim Sugar/Corbis; page 101, right; © Owen Franken/Corbis; page 102, © Larry Banares/World Talk Radio; page 106, © Jim Davey/Multi Media Productions, Inc.; page 110, © Larry Williams/Corbis; page 117, top left; © Hulton-Deutsch Collection/Corbis; page 117, bottom left; © Bettmann/Corbis; page 117, right; © Bill Gentile/Corbis; page 118, © Jeanne Markle; page 122, ©Carol Guzy/The Washington Post; page 125, © Tomika Perdomo; page 133, top; © Inga Spence/Getty Images; page 133, bottom left; © Lee White/Corbis; page 133, bottom right; © Darrell Gulin/Corbis; page 134, © Hulton Archive/Getty Images; page 138, © Associated Press; page 142, © Ramin Talaie/Corbis